BIRTH RECORDS COUNSELLING

a practical guide

Published by
British Agencies for
Adoption & Fostering
11 Southwark Street
London SE1 1RQ

© BAAF 1991

ISBN 0 903534 97 5

Designed by Alastair Whitson
Typeset by Intertype
Printed and bound in England by
The College Hill Press Limited

The cover design features a specimen
copy of a birth certificate (as issued to
people born after 1967). BAAF is grateful for permission to reproduce this
specimen certificate, which is Crown
copyright: reproduced with the permission of the Controller of Her Majesty's
Stationary Office.

BIRTH RECORDS COUNSELLING

a practical guide

by Pam Hodgkins

British Agencies for Adoption & Fostering

About the author

Pam Hodgkins has extensive experience in counselling and working with adopted people and adoptive and birth parents and relatives. She has also conducted and published research into the outcome of adoption reunions. She is now employed as Consultant (Child Placement) at the BAAF Midlands Regional Centre, and she also provides training on a freelance basis on birth records counselling and other post-adoption services.

Acknowledgements

I would like to thank the director and staff of the Post-Adoption Centre, Georgina Stafford of BAAF, Linda Savell of NORCAP and Cathy Swanson of Coventry Social Services for sharing with me their experiences of birth records counselling and for making very useful suggestions, comments and constructive criticism about this guide at every stage of its development. In addition, Janys Scott of BAAF's Scottish Centre and Linda Paterson of Family Care have supplied helpful information about practice in Scotland.

I would also like to thank my husband and the editors at BAAF for helping me to convert some training programme notes into a practical guide for counsellors.

Pam Hodgkins

Contents

Part 1   Introduction

Adopted adults in England and Wales were finally given the right to access to their birth records in 1976 – nearly 50 years after the right was introduced in Scotland. Yet, despite the Scottish experience, the introduction of this right in England and Wales was highly controversial and represented a major change in public thinking about adoption.

Many people believed that it would provide the first opportunity for any adopted person to discover their original identity. This widely held belief was of course incorrect. Adoptive parents have usually been aware of the birth details of their child, and many have been willing to share what information they have with their son or daughter at an appropriate time. The introduction of a statutory entitlement to birth details simply ensured that all adopted adults in England and Wales had the same opportunity to discover their original identity and were no longer subject to the will, and the ability to remember, of their adoptive parents.

When Parliament debated giving access to birth records much concern was expressed that birth mothers might be located and their present lives destroyed by the appearance of their 'child from the past'. Many adoption workers in England and Wales had assured women who gave their baby for adoption that they would never have any contact with the child again: the child would never be able to trace them, they would never be able to trace the child, and so they should put it all behind them.

Workers and agencies which had followed that line, unaware that it was untrue even when stated, were most anxious for their former clients and afraid of breaking past undertakings. To placate all those concerned the concept of 'compulsory counselling' was introduced into the legislation: anyone adopted before the access to birth records provision was introduced would only be given their original birth details after attending a counselling interview (counselling is available but not compulsory for those adopted after the provision was introduced).

It was intended that the counselling interview would include warning the adopted person that tracing their birth parent may cause distress. The counsellor would explain to the adopted person the climate of secrecy that had surrounded adoption for many years and advise them to be discreet and cautious in any approach. In some cases this meant that the adopted person was being kindly, but firmly, 'warned off'. In effect a double message was being given to adopted people: they were entitled by law to the information, but the counselling implied that to use it may be unwise.

Yet the law itself is clear and precise: having attended a counselling interview as required, an adopted adult is then entitled to receive the information which would enable her or him to purchase a certified copy of the record of her or his birth (normally referred to as 'the original birth certificate'). Counsellors must remember that adopted adults have the right to make their own decisions about how they use this information. The counselling role is an enabling and informing one: the aim is not to discourage adopted people, but rather to ensure that they are fully aware of the possible implications for themselves and others of tracing their birth parent or birth family.

Using this guide

This book has been written to provide some practical assistance for social workers required to provide birth records counselling to adopted adults. It will also be useful to any counsellor working with an adopted person considering contact with birth relatives.

The issues and topics covered reflect the concerns of adopted people and it is hoped that the suggestions included here will enable the counsellor to meet effectively the expectations of the adopted person. In addition the book covers issues raised by social workers – both practical queries and fundamental questions of professional practice.

The legal position is outlined at the beginning of the next section, *Background details*. The rest of that section is based on the legal position in England and Wales, but the counselling issues are relevant everywhere. The section looks at what the adopted person may wish to know and their reasons for wishing to gain that information, and the role of the counsellor,

including guidelines for assessing to what extent counsellors should assist adopted people in tracing their birth parents. This is followed by some case studies which give an idea of the variety of situations that birth records counsellors can face. The case studies will be particularly useful for workers who are new to birth records counselling.

The next section focuses on the first interview. It takes as its basis the statutory interview required in England and Wales under section 51 of the 1976 Adoption Act (which can also be taken as the model for an interview required in Northern Ireland under article 54 of the Adoption (NI) Order 1987). It is intended to supplement and expand on areas covered in the Department of Health publication *Access to birth records: notes for counsellors*, a copy of which is issued by the Registrar General with every set of papers concerning an application for birth records information.

It is important that all counsellors appreciate that they cannot be certain that there will be more than one opportunity to discuss key issues with an adopted person who has applied for birth records counselling. It must also be understood, when providing counselling under section 51 or article 54, that the adopted person has a right to the statutory information by the completion of the first interview, any further sessions being by mutual agreement.

The legal position in Scotland is different to that in England, Wales and Northern Ireland (see below for details), but much of the practical guidance in the section on *The first interview* also applies to birth records counselling requested by adopted people in Scotland. Differences in procedure are referred to where appropriate, and separate checklists are given for interviews carried out under the Scottish provision. The main difference is that the adopted person will probably have already received their birth records information, and so this does not need to be handed over during the interview.

Subsequent sections of the book – on *Searching* and *Making contact* – will be useful to all workers involved in birth records counselling, as they deal with ongoing counselling for adopted people who are interested in tracing and perhaps making contact with their birth relatives.

Following discussion of each stage of the process there is a checklist summarising the main points. These checklists are collected in Appendix 4, which can be photocopied and kept with each client's papers as a handy reference.

Throughout the book the aim is to highlight issues and difficulties which may arise and suggest ways in which counsellors can help their clients to overcome any problems they encounter. The following chart illustrates the process by which an application for birth records information is made and the various paths it may take after the initial counselling interview. This chart is a useful reference, but it is important to remember that every request for birth records counselling should be treated as an individual case. Counsellors must be flexible and prepared to adapt the process described in this book according to the circumstances, wishes and needs of the adopted person.

Whilst the initial expectation was that an application for birth records information would result in a single interview, in practice most counsellors now anticipate working with the adopted person over a longer period. The suggestions made in this book are intended to cover an extended piece of work.

Flow chart of birth records counselling process

based on application for birth records information under section 51 of the Adoption Act 1976 (England and Wales)

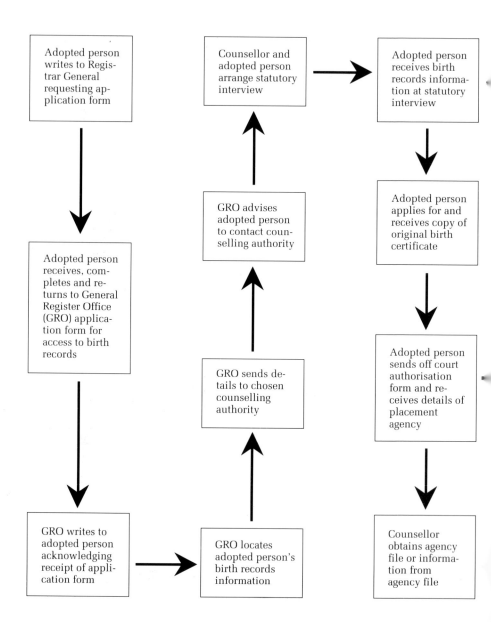

normal line of developments
possible alternative routes of progress (eg if adopted person carries out search without further counselling)

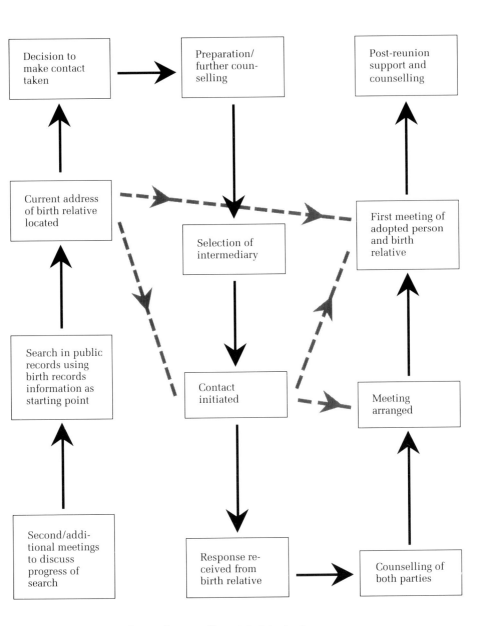

The legal position

Adopted adults in **England and Wales** were given a right of access to their birth records by an amendment to the 1958 Adoption Act contained in section 26 of the 1975 Children Act. This clause came into effect one year after the passing of the Act, in November 1976. The access to birth records provisions also formed part of the 1976 Adoption Act which was finally fully implemented on 1 January 1988.

The legislation concerning access to birth records is contained in section 51 of the Adoption Act 1976, under which adopted people aged 18 or over are entitled to:
- birth records information (including their original name and that of their birth mother) that will enable them to obtain a copy of their original birth certificate
- authorisation to obtain from the court which granted the adoption order the name of the adoption society or local authority (if any) which took part in the adoption proceedings.

Anyone adopted before the provision was introduced (12 November 1975, when the 1975 Children Act was passed) must attend a counselling interview, at which they will receive the above information. Counselling is available but not compulsory for those adopted on or after 12 November 1975.

Provision similar to that in England and Wales was introduced in **Northern Ireland** under article 54 of the Adoption (Northern Ireland) Order 1987, which came into force on 1 October 1989. The information supplied is the same, but in Northern Ireland counselling is compulsory for those who were adopted before 18 December 1987.

In **Scotland**, adopted people have had a right of access to their records since 1930. This provision is now set out in section 45 of the Adoption (Scotland) Act 1978, under which any adopted person aged 17 or over is entitled to information about and a copy or extract of their original birth entry. There is no obligation on the adopted person to seek counselling, and counselling is never a precondition of obtaining information. However, when this information is given to an adopted person, the Registrar General must also advise him or her that counselling services are available from the local authority for the area in which they live, or if their adoption was arranged by an adoption society, from that society. The local authority or adoption society is obliged to provide counselling for people who have received information about their birth entry and who apply for counselling.

In addition, the **Children Act 1989**, which is in effect from 14 October 1991, contains important amendments which provide that adopted people living in the United Kingdom who apply for birth records information under section 51, article 54 or section 45 above, can choose to receive counselling from the local authority (or health and social services board in Northern Ireland) for the area in which they live. This means that, for example, someone who was adopted in England but is now living in Scotland, and who applies for their birth records information to the Registrar General for England and Wales, can receive the information at a birth records counselling interview at their local authority in Scotland.

A further important amendment under the 1989 Children Act concerns adopted people who now live outside the UK but were adopted in England or Wales and apply for birth records information under section 51 of the 1976 Adoption Act. If they were adopted before 12 November 1975 they must attend a counselling interview before they can receive the information, but this interview can now be provided by any body approved by the Registrar General – such as an adoption society or counselling agency – in the country in which the adopted person is now living.

The effect of these amendments is that a social worker or counsellor anywhere in the world could conceivably be asked to provide birth records counselling!

Why adopted people want to know about their origins

Most people need to know who they are. For the majority their identity is never in question. They grow up surrounded by their roots, frequently seeing likenesses to themselves in other family members and having their sense of personal history continually reinforced by normal conversations within their family. Adopted people cannot take their history for granted in the same way, yet like everyone else they were born: their life did not begin at the time they were placed with their adoptive family. For some adopted people life story books will contain the factual details of their life, but that informal, personal recollection and anecdote is still missing. For those people adopted as infants many years ago, details of what happened to them before they were adopted are often not available. It is this need to know, to explain oneself, to close a significant gap, which triggers in many adopted people an application for birth records counselling.

The Department of Health booklet *Access to birth records: notes for counsellors* has changed little since its original publication. It appears it was greatly influenced by the research of John Triseliotis in Scotland* which suggested that:
• only unhappy or dissatisfied adopted people will want to search
• useful ongoing relationships between adopted people and birth relatives are most unusual
• seeking access to birth records is a minority response to being adopted.

However this research was conducted in the late 1960s and since access to birth records was introduced in England and Wales in 1975 some further studies have been conducted.† These

* *In search of origins* Routledge & Kegan Paul, 1973
† Day C and Leeding A *Access to birth records* ABAFA, 1980
Haimes E and Timms N *Adoption, identity and social policy* Gower, 1985
Hodgkins P *Adopted adults – their relationships with their birth and adoptive families* NORCAP, 1987

studies – supported by the experience of specialist agencies like the National Organisation for the Counselling of Adoptees and Parents (NORCAP) and the Post-Adoption Centre – indicate:

• applicants for birth records counselling express various opinions about adoption

• the need to know about origins relates to an individual's concept of self-identity rather than to any external pressures

• useful and satisfying relationships do develop between adopted adults and members of their birth family

• careful interpretation of the official statistics in England and Wales (with appropriate allowances for the number of 'in family' adoptions and for the number of individuals who can obtain their original birth certificates without having to use the section 51 provision) suggests that over 50 per cent of women and 30 per cent of men adopted outside their birth family will make some enquiries to trace their family of origin.

In some cases adopted people who have applied to receive their birth records information are very clear about how far they wish to proceed; in others they may be less certain. But whatever their intentions, adopted people are unlikely to have made their application lightly, and the need to know about their origins can take on considerable importance in their life.

The role of the counsellor

The booklet *Access to birth records: notes for counsellors* stresses the need to warn adopted people of the likelihood of a hostile response from any traced birth parent and encourages respect for the birth parent's privacy. This was the key function of the compulsory counselling in England and Wales: to offer some degree of protection and so encourage Parliament to make the provision for access to birth records for adopted people retrospective. With the benefit of hindsight it can now be seen to be equally important to prepare the adopted person for an immediate and overwhelming welcome from the birth parent. Adopted people should also be warned of the risk that they may lose their own privacy once contact has been renewed.

However, as every social worker will be aware, advising and warning are not the key elements of counselling. Workers will want to bring to the task counselling skills which enable the adopted person to feel relaxed and to talk freely and openly in the knowledge that the counsellor is not judging them but trying to empathise with their situation and their experience of adoption. Counselling should enable adopted people to clarify their feelings about their own adoption and their expectations about their birth family, express their doubts and fears, and move towards achieving a solution that they will be able to live with comfortably.

The counsellor does have a responsibility to represent to the adopted person the interests of other people involved, but this should always be done on the basis of researched facts and not assumptions. Despite the warning about the number of women who placed babies for adoption many years ago who wait in fear of being traced, it has been found that there are at least an equal number who spend every day hoping and longing to be reunited with their son or daughter. The majority will fall between these two extreme responses.

Helping adopted people to trace birth parents

If an applicant for birth records counselling does want to seek out their birth parents, how much time should the social worker allocate to assisting them? Can the allocation of any time be justified? It is interesting work to do – a welcome change from most social work tasks – and inside many a social worker lurks an amateur Sherlock Holmes, waiting to be unleashed. But is family research on behalf of an adult an appropriate use of time for a social worker, especially in an agency where time is one of the most limited resources?

A helpful comparison here is with a request for benefit advice. How would a social worker handle that? They would probably:
1 Provide guidelines for the client – a DSS leaflet.
2 Put the client in touch with the appropriate specialists, eg a welfare rights centre.
3 Assist the client with any specific difficulties – especially where this will include the teaching of a useful skill such as letter writing or form completion.
4 Reassure the client that further help will be available should they encounter any difficulties.

The same philosophy can be applied to a request for birth records counselling:
1 The applicant for counselling could be given some guidelines on how to search – for example, they could be advised to purchase a copy of *Searching for family connections* published by NORCAP (see Appendix 2 for details).
2 The applicant should be advised that there are specialist agencies available to assist them. NORCAP assists and supports adopted adults during and after their search and can provide detailed searching advice. In addition, a 'Recordscan' research service is available to members of NORCAP at the Gen-

eral Register Office and other London public record offices, and assistance with searches that lead overseas can often be provided. The Post-Adoption Centre and Post Adoption Services provide a specialist counselling service and opportunities for group therapy sessions. In Scotland, the Scottish Adoption Advice Service and the Adoption Counselling Centre specialise in counselling for anyone involved in adoption, including adopted people who are considering tracing their origins. (See Appendix 1 for details and addresses.)
3 If the applicant is helped to conduct their own search they will be left with a sense of achievement even if the final outcome is not as they might wish. They will have gained confidence in approaching officials, using public records, and lateral thinking – all skills which may be of lasting benefit to them.
4 The applicant should be assured that they can turn to the social worker at any time if they encounter any difficulties. The social worker can also use his or her specialist skills and connections to obtain and interpret information for the applicant.

Using guidelines like these to determine when and how to help should ensure that the social worker directs his or her time to those areas where it is most needed.

Some case studies

The following case studies are a compilation of circumstances drawn from the actual experiences of counsellors; some features and responses are drawn from the experiences of adopted people. They are not the individual stories of three people but contain collected features from scores of people. It is important that they are read as examples of what *may* happen. They should not be taken to suggest what *should* happen, as none is intended as an example of good practice – indeed, included in the case studies are some glaring (and some subtle) examples of bad practice. These are included to help counsellors appreciate that their best intentions may be misinterpreted or cause unforeseen difficulties. In particular, it is hoped that readers will be aware that birth records counselling is a bridging process: whether one identifies with the work done many years ago or tries to distance oneself from it, the past will cast its shadow over the present piece of work. The adopted person has made the application because they want the past unlocked; counsellors must share that experience with them and they, too, may find it painful.

These brief summaries also show that, whilst planning is important, the counsellor will never know with any certainty what may happen next or for how long and to what extent the adopted person will require assistance.

'Owen'

The information about Owen supplied by the General Register Office was very limited. The social worker, Tim, had received only the birth certificate information which indicated Owen was 29, and the court application form authorising disclosure of the name of the adoption agency which had arranged Owen's adoption. Owen had asked to receive counselling at his local social services office which was in an industrial midlands town ('Midtown'). Tim arranged to meet Owen first thing one morning. Owen was anxious not to be too late for work but Tim had explained they would probably need to talk for about an hour.

When Owen arrived, Tim examined the identification offered, a passbook to the Rhonda Building Society, which Owen explained was the only official thing he had with his current address as he had only moved to Midtown from Wales a couple of months ago.

Tim began by inviting Owen to tell him what he already knew about his adoption. Owen's information was scant: his Mam had often talked about going to Cardiff to the big office of the Chapel headquarters to collect him, and what a tiny scrap of a baby he had been. He said his Mam had asked where he had come from but the sister in charge had said his background was fine and they should not worry, just begin from today. Owen understood he was seven weeks old at that time. He added that he had not asked questions very often, mainly because it had never seemed that important.

They talked briefly about Owen's childhood which appeared to have been quite happy and normal. He had been close to both his parents, especially to his mother after his father was killed in a pit accident several years ago. The family had lived in the same house in a village between Brecon and Merthyr throughout his childhood, and Owen had been brought up to be bilingual.

Tim asked Owen if anything in particular had prompted his application. It transpired that the move to Midtown was a key factor as Owen thought he would make enquiries 'just to satisfy his normal curiosity' whilst he was away from Wales. He explained that he was working in Midtown for two years on secondment and that although he was glad of the opportunity to 'see how the rest of the world lives' he and his family were pleased it was only a temporary move. They had let their house which was only five minutes' walk from Owen's mother's, and would return there just before his elder son would be five and ready to start at Owen's old school.

Glancing at his watch Owen asked Tim if he could have the information. Tim sorted through the papers he held and began to say 'I think this is what you are most keen to know ...' when it suddenly dawned on him that he was talking to a Welshman, a man as Welsh as daffodils and leeks, and look what he had to tell him. His name had been registered as George Andrew Smith, son of Rose Smith, and the birth had been registered in London. There was no Welsh connection whatsoever. How would Owen cope with having been George?

Tim paused. 'I expect you thought you had been born in Wales?' he asked. 'Well, yes' replied Owen, sensing Tim's uncertainty. Tim explained that Owen had been born in London, and that his mother was Rose Smith. He handed the yellow paper to Owen and said 'she named you George Andrew'. Owen looked a little taken aback but managed to joke, 'I expect she thought it was suitable for someone who might have to slay dragons.' Tim felt that he had somehow failed Owen in this apparently simple piece of work, but he could not change the facts. Was there any way of making them more acceptable?

Owen looked at his watch again which reminded Tim of what he had to cover in the remaining time. He asked Owen what he thought he would do next. Owen said he would send for his birth certificate and that he might write to the court as his mother had never been

very clear as to which agency was involved, always referring to 'the Chapel headquarters'. Tim asked Owen to be careful not to do anything which might upset Rose and to feel he could always contact him for extra help or suggestions. Owen was by now sitting on the edge of his chair, but assured Tim he had no intention of getting in touch with Rose and would give him a ring if anything turned up. Tim handed Owen the court authorisation form and they shook hands.

Tim had two phone calls from Owen. The first was to let him know that the birth certificate had arrived and to enquire after the records of a now closed agency. Tim referred to the reference book *Where to find adoption records** and advised Owen of the address of the record holder.

A few weeks later Owen phoned again. He had been to see the social worker in London and learned that he was the child of a young unmarried mother and that his father, although unnamed, was a near neighbour of the same age. Both families had felt adoption of the baby was the best option. Owen guessed Tim's unspoken question. 'I only finished up in Cardiff as there were so many baby boys that summer that the agency had run out of people wanting boys, so six of us were taken to Wales,' said Owen. Tim asked him what he planned to do next. 'Nothing,' replied Owen, 'I've satisfied my curiosity and any more would be tempting providence – but thanks for your help.'

---

* *Where to find adoption records* compiled by Georgina Stafford (BAAF, 1985) lists details of voluntary adoption agencies, social services departments, maternity, mother-and-baby and shelter homes, and details of the current location and availability of their records.

'Katie'

Katie applied for access to her birth records just weeks after her 18th birthday. The papers were sent by the adoption unit at County Hall to Margaret, a social worker recently returned after a career break, at the local office in the Borders. Margaret was apprehensive. There was no file and the birth had been in Bolton, where the adoption also took place when Katie was 18 months old.

Margaret had been an adoption worker in the sixties. She was not sure she agreed with this new idea of adopted people finding their original families. She could remember promising so many mothers that once they had handed over the baby and signed the affidavit for the magistrate that would be the end of the matter. She had encouraged young women to build new lives free from the shadow of illegitimacy; now she was being asked to undermine them.

She wrote to Katie and suggested she visited her at home one afternoon. Katie rang Margaret: she wanted the interview at the office; if Margaret came to the house her Mum would find out. Margaret was firm – the office was being painted, there was nowhere available for meetings, and anyhow Katie should have told her mother. Katie gave in and Margaret called as arranged.

A middle-aged white woman answered the door and showed Margaret in to the lounge. She said she would call Katie, who was being 'a bit difficult as she is worried about today'. As the woman started to leave Margaret motioned to her to stay and whispered: 'What do you think about this, will she cause trouble?' The woman moved away,

saying: 'It is not for me to decide what Katie does. She has to sort herself out.'

Katie came in. Margaret could hardly conceal her surprise: Katie was black. Margaret began her prepared speech. She had come to give Katie the information she was legally entitled to receive, but before she did so she must warn Katie that her mother would not be expecting to hear from her, her mother may be afraid of her turning up, her family may not know anything about Katie, and if she wasn't careful she, Katie, could cause havoc. Perhaps it would be better if Katie waited until she was older – she may be better able to cope then and her real mother might have had more time to find out that she may be traced.

Katie pointed at her adoptive mother and said: 'She is my real mother. The woman on that form you're holding gave me away because I was black. My father was black. I want to find my father.' Margaret was lost for words.

Katie asked Margaret whether she had any information that would help her find her father. Margaret shuffled her papers and explained that would be very difficult as Katie was illegitimate and so her father may not have been named on the birth certificate. 'I think that if you really want to go through with this I had better trace your mother and see if she can give us any information,' she said. 'It will be safer all round that way. I will let you know what she says.' She thought back to her instructions. 'Do you want me to give you the information about your name and where you were born now?' she said. 'Of course not,' retorted Katie. 'Mum has always told me I was originally called Catherine, after some saint or other, and her name was Janice Wheeler. I was born at Bolton Infirmary, so if that's all you have to tell me I already know it all. I only started this to find out about my father, so now you know who to find!'

Katie strode out of the room and her mother looked apologetically at Margaret. 'I hope you can find him. It is important to her but it won't be easy – I understand he was a Ghanaian student,' she said. She explained to Margaret that she had two sons and had always wanted a daughter, but had high blood pressure in her last pregnancy and was advised to have no more children. At that time her neighbour did fostering and had a beautiful baby girl who did not go for adoption at six weeks like the other babies the neighbour fostered because she was not 'all white' and 'no one wanted to adopt a baby like that'. So she had persuaded her husband that they should adopt the little girl, Katie, and the next time the welfare woman came her neighbour invited her in to chat about it. The welfare department first checked with Katie's mother who was quite relieved as she had been told her daughter would be unadoptable. The department then checked out the family, and soon Katie became theirs.

A few days later Margaret requested the agency file from Bolton to see if this could give her any more information. From this she learned that Katie's birth mother had gone back to her managerial job in Surrey soon after the adoption had been arranged. From a letter in the file she also learned the address of the mother's parents' home.

Margaret checked the phone books at the library and found that someone with Janice's family name, Griffin, still lived at the address. She wrote to Jan-

ice there, c/o Mr A Griffin, the name in the phone book. Inside was a typed letter asking Janice to contact her to resolve a problem concerning the child she had had adopted in 1962.

When the letter arrived Mr Griffin rang Janice who said she did not know anyone in the Borders. Curious, she asked him to read the letter to her – and heard his sudden intake of breath. Her father did not know she had ever had a child. Janice drove straight down to see him. Her father looked drawn and grey. He asked: 'Did your mother know?'

Janice felt very angry but also sad, as she felt she had gone down in her father's estimation. Then she recalled she had read an article in a magazine about a group that helped with these events. The next day she phoned NORCAP and talked for over an hour to a volunteer who understood her anger at the approach, her guilt that had surfaced, and her need to establish what the problem was without having contact with the signatory of the letter, whom she was inclined to murder!

NORCAP offered to try and sort things out. A NORCAP counsellor contacted Margaret and explained what havoc her well-intentioned letter had caused. Margaret was unwilling to relinquish her control of the case but agreed to pass on a letter from NORCAP asking Katie to contact them if she wished.

Katie responded to this letter, talked at length to a NORCAP counsellor and attended some group discussions. By talking to other people in the group with similar histories Katie had found her bitterness towards her birth mother diminished and a meeting between them was arranged through an intermediary. Katie was pleased to learn that

Janice had remarried quite recently to a black man and that when they eventually met he seemed to Katie to be the first person who really appreciated what her life was like. Katie found she made many new friends through Janice and her husband and for the first time found herself mixing with people from many different ethnic backgrounds.

Janice rang to check Katie was home safely after a visit to London and talked to Katie's adoptive mother. They found they had a lot in common, not least concern for Katie and a shared intent to help her put the difficulties of the past behind her and fulfil her potential. Both women were with Katie on her wedding day four years later. Katie still plans to trace her father 'some day' but it is no longer an immediate priority in her life.

'Sarah'

Sarah had requested birth records counselling from the authority which also happened to hold her adoption papers. As a result the GRO's papers arrived at the area office clipped to the department's file on the adoption.

Angela was allocated the work and settled down to read the file. It was unusual to have all the information: the mother's file, the baby file and the file on the adopters had all been merged. It took Angela some time to organise all the papers chronologically.

Sarah's name seemed familiar and when Angela checked her address she found that it was a few doors away from a couple whose assessment she had just finished. She suddenly remembered that Sarah had been one of their referees. Angela wrote inviting Sarah to come into the office and received a note acknowledging the appointment.

Prior to the interview Angela sorted the papers, prepared a summary and had two copies typed up. Sarah's adoption was typical of the late 1950s: she was the child of a 22-year-old unmarried secretary who had had a brief affair with her boss. Faced with her pregnancy he had given her £50 and her cards. The mother, Joan, had moved into a mother and baby home in a neighbouring town and had placed her baby for adoption through a local agency which had closed some years ago.

The agency had kept meticulous records and so the files handed on to the local authority were comprehensive. There was correspondence from Joan on the file, which Angela removed and replaced with photocopies, and also a photo of a young woman holding a tiny baby; on the back was written 'Baby no 261/58 with mother'. There was a final letter from Joan to the agency acknowledging receipt of her notification that an adoption order had been granted and stating that she now had a good job with a local council and had become engaged to one of the trainee accountants. Joan added that they planned to marry next summer.

Sarah arrived early for the interview. She produced a whole envelope full of documents when asked for her identification and did not acknowledge that she had met Angela before. Angela asked: 'You are Sarah who I visited about Mike and Carol aren't you?' Sarah relaxed a little and smiled. 'Yes,' she replied, 'that was the start of all this really.' She went on to explain that she had been very involved in her friends' plans to become adoptive parents; over coffee Carol would tell Sarah all about the group meeting she and Mike had attended the night before and later had used Sarah as a sounding board as she tried to work out what she really felt about issues Angela raised whilst doing their assessment. Sarah told Angela how she had supported Carol through all the lengthy tests when she could not become pregnant and how she had watched them gradually reach the decision to try and adopt. 'But I told you all that when you visited me,' she concluded. Angela smiled: 'You did not tell me you were adopted.'

'No,' replied Sarah, 'I wasn't sure if you would see that as a good thing or not. You might have thought it made me biased. I only told Carol a couple of weeks back when they heard they had been accepted by the adoption panel; but it made me do a lot of thinking.' Sarah explained that the information about birth parents from the prospective adopters' group meetings which Carol discussed had made her realise that somewhere she had a mother who might be concerned about her and anxious for information. She had decided it was her responsibility to find out.

Angela acknowledged all that Sarah had said before pointing out the different climate of opinion that existed 30 years ago. She suggested that, whilst Sarah's birth mother might want news of her, she would have been told adoption was the end of her involvement. Unlike the birth parent of any child Carol and Mike may adopt, Sarah's mother would not have been prepared for the possibility of contact in years to come. 'She may not welcome it,' warned Angela. Sarah said she did appreciate that things used to be different and she was quite prepared to accept whatever her mother wanted, but she felt it was her duty to find out.

She asked if Angela had any information that might help her find her moth-

er. Angela told her of the thick file, explained she had summarised the information, and asked if Sarah wanted her to go through it. Sarah assured her that she was anxious to have every possible detail.

As Angela read through her notes Sarah made comments about what she already knew from her adoptive parents, who had both died some years before, and expressed surprise at some new information, including her time of birth which her adoptive mother had never known. Angela explained about the letters and photograph on file. 'May I see them?' asked Sarah. Angela replied that not only could she see them but she could keep them if she wished. Sarah's face lit up. Even being known as 'Baby 261/58' did not remove the smile.

Angela talked with Sarah about how she planned to try and locate Joan. Sarah intended to see if she could find any local sources first whilst waiting for her birth certificate to come. She agreed with Angela on the importance of an intermediary and promised to keep Angela up to date with her progress.

Angela expected to hear from Sarah but not quite so soon as she did. Early the next afternoon Sarah rang to say she knew where Joan was living and would Angela please contact her. It emerged that Sarah had gone to the City Library and combed through back issues of the local paper until she found the report of Joan's wedding the summer after her adoption. This gave her Joan's married name and confirmed that she had married a municipal accountant; it also gave the area of the couple's new home. Sarah located their address from the old registers of electors and checked each year until 1972 when they were no longer listed. Undeterred she checked the telephone directories for the whole country and came up with 73 possible entries.

She had spent the whole morning on the telephone to town halls the length and breadth of Britain checking these addresses with current registers of electors. Only one, in a town some 30 miles away, had both Joan's name and her husband's name; a Martin Peter was also listed. Fired on by her success Sarah had asked if the clerk knew of a Mr Michael James Gregory (Joan's husband) in accounts. 'Oh yes,' was the reply, 'Mr Gregory is our Borough Treasurer.' Sarah rushed back to the library reference section and checked the Municipal Year Book. There before her was the confirmation: M J Gregory, Treasurer from 1972. A further check with the Accountants' Year Book listed M J Gregory as having been articled at Worcester City Council 1954-59, Accountant 1959-67, Assistant City Treasurer 1967-72, and Treasurer Swandale Borough from 1972.

Angela invited Sarah to meet with her later that week. 'You have waited thirty years, now it has all happened at once it won't hurt to wait a few more days,' Angela said. 'Give yourself a chance to take it all in; go and talk things over with Carol.'

Sarah arrived at the office laden with papers. She had checked everything: her research was meticulous. She had also read everything she could lay her hands on about post-adoption reunions in the intervening two days. She seemed to know more than Angela did, but they both benefited from a long and involved discussion.

Angela agreed to write to Joan, adding that she would send Sarah a copy at the same time so Sarah would have an idea when the letter would arrive. Sarah could contact Angela whenever she needed but Angela would only ring Sarah when she had heard from Joan. Sarah hoped Joan would want to meet her quickly. She had established that the Gregorys had two sons but that Joan had never had another daughter. Knowing that Sarah had been born Joanne Mitchell, Angela wrote:

Dear Mrs Gregory,
   I wonder if you can help me. I have had an enquiry from a woman, Joanne, who is trying to contact family members she lost touch with some time ago. She has established a connection to the Mitchell family and as your maiden name was Mitchell we wondered if you may be able to help?
   We both realise that there are many Mitchells in Worcester but I believe you used to live in the city. Incidentally Joanne is 31 and she was born in Severnbridge, which as you may know is just a few miles from Worcester.
   If you think you can help could you please give me a ring or drop me a line. I am normally in my office until 10.15 each morning. I look forward to hearing from you.
   Yours sincerely
   Angela Smith
   Senior Social Worker.

She had to get the letter retyped as her secretary put her normal designation, area adoption officer, on the first one.

She only had to wait two days for the reply. Joan Gregory was as direct and thorough as her daughter. She acknowledged that she was the person Joanne was looking for but asked if Angela had made a mistake as she believed Joanne was now called Sarah. She admitted she had expected to be found. She had read about the change in the law but when nothing happened for over ten years she assumed her daughter was not interested.

Angela filled her in with some details of Sarah's life. Joan asked if Sarah could be patient for a short while. She explained that her elder son was to be married soon, and whilst it might seem fairy-tale stuff she did not feel she could cope with regaining a daughter at the same time as losing a son; anyway she wanted their first contact to be just for them, not in the midst of her own and someone else's family. 'Please tell Sarah I am glad she has found me,' she added before ringing off.

Sarah was delighted with the news but later revealed to Angela that she was glad of Carol's support as she kept bursting into tears even though she felt happy. After Angela had arranged an exchange of photographs and letters Sarah and Joan met at Birmingham International station just over two weeks later. After an hour they were joined by Michael and lunched together. The meeting went very well, and Sarah met her half-brothers a few weeks later.

Part 3   The first interview

The counsellor needs to be aware that this may be the only interview. It should be appreciated that applicants for birth records counselling may not be completely frank about their aims and intentions. The prime aim of applicants in England and Wales may be to pass what they see as a test of suitability and obtain their birth details. Of course, there is no test of suitability involved, but unless this is clearly stated to applicants they may well misinterpret the situation and be careful about their responses.

It is the counsellor's responsibility to ensure that applicants leave the first interview aware that the counsellor will be available to help them in the future. The counsellor must also decide the extent to which the information to hand is shared at this stage. Responsibility must be accepted not only for the consequences of sharing information but also for the consequences that result from not sharing information.

The ethnic background of the adopted person

Careful consideration should be given to the ethnic background of the applicant. Wherever possible an applicant should have the opportunity to have the interview provided by a counsellor from the same ethnic background. Racial identity is an integral part of an individual's total identity, and the adopted person's need for full knowl-

edge of their own identity is the key factor in an application for access to birth records. It is therefore essential for the applicant to be seen by a worker whom they can perceive as understanding all the issues that relate to their sense of identity.

This is particularly important when it is known or is possible that the applicant was adopted transracially, in order that any issues which may affect either the applicant or the sought parents can be sensitively addressed. Workers providing counselling in these circumstances will find it useful to read the Post-Adoption Centre's discussion paper *A glimpse through the looking glass: a summary of personal experiences and reflections of a group of transracially adopted adults.** This short paper offers poignant insights into how transracially adopted people's intense need for defining their 'self' can lead to an intense desire to find family connections. The paper also emphasises that transracially adopted adults can feel even more acutely some of the anxieties felt by all adopted people preparing to search: a reluctance to approach agencies for fear of having judgements made about their motiva-

---

* Shekleton J *A glimpse through the looking glass* Post-Adoption Centre Discussion Paper No 8, September 1990. BAAF is grateful for permission to refer to some of the points raised by this discussion paper.

tion to search; questioning of their own right to know about their past, and generally needing reassurance that it is normal to want to know; and a suspicion that they have to pass some sort of test of stability, and that expressing the desire for information about their past would be interpreted as unstable (ie that they have not integrated into their adoptive family).

Arranging the first interview

Applications for birth records information are made to the Registrar General (see Appendix 1 for address). On receipt of the initial enquiry the Registrar General sends the applicant a copy of the leaflet *Access to birth records: information for adopted people*, and a form on which they are asked to give details of themselves which will enable their records to be located. They also have to indicate their choice of counselling location. This can be the General Register Office in London, a social services department or, if known, the adoption agency involved.

The Registrar General acknowledges receipt of this form and advises the applicant when he has transmitted the counselling request and relevant papers to the named authority. Some applicants immediately contact the counselling agency; others wait for the counsellor to contact them. To assist in building confidence between the applicant and the counsellor a prompt acknowledgement of receipt of the papers should be given, and a brief explanation offered if there is to be an unavoidable delay before an interview can be arranged.

The interview should be held in hospitable surroundings and be free from interruptions. The applicant is likely to be nervous: there is a frequent assumption that the purpose of the interview is to determine if they are fit to be given the information. To overcome this it may be helpful when arranging the appointment to outline to the applicant the nature of the counselling sessions. Pointing out that a friend or relative is welcome to come along as well is further reassurance of the non-testing climate of the interview. Reassure the applicant that any papers or information they already hold will be useful and that, in addition to sharing the formal birth records information, there will be plenty of opportunity to discuss any points they raise. Do emphasise that applicants *will* receive their birth details during this interview.

As with all interviews, when a client has an appointment to see a worker at a specific time it is important to be punctual or to send a message to explain any really unavoidable delay, along with a clear indication of how long the delay is likely to be.

Adopted people in Scotland apply for birth records information to the General Register Office in Edinburgh (see Appendix 1 for address). The Registrar General sends the information direct to the adopted person, and advises them that counselling services are available if they wish. In Scotland the request for counselling will therefore come direct from the adopted person. As they will probably already have obtained their birth records information, it is likely that they will be seeking counselling in connection with that information and advice as to steps they might take to secure further information.

Preparing for the first interview

The counsellor in England and Wales will receive the following papers from the Registrar General:

- a copy of the leaflet *Access to birth records: information for adopted people*
- a copy of the leaflet *Access to birth records: notes for counsellors*
- a copy of the adopted person's application for counselling (endorsed with the name of the court which made the adoption order and the number of the adoption application)
- a form containing the applicant's birth records information, including their original name and that of their birth parents. This form can then be used by the applicant to obtain a copy of their original birth certificate
- a court authorisation form to enable the applicant to obtain from the court the name of the adoption agency or local authority which took part in the adoption proceedings
- a form to be signed by the counsellor and returned to the Registrar General to show that counselling has taken place.

(The counsellor will also be told if a relative of the adopted person has registered with the Adoption Contact Register set up by the Children Act 1989 – see the section on *Adoption contact registers*, page 32, for further details.)

These papers may include sufficient information for you to identify the placement agency (for example, the adopted person may already know the name of the placement agency and have indicated this on their form). If so, it would be advisable to contact that agency to establish if there has been any contact with the birth parent or other family member since the adoption order was made. If the placement agency is no longer operating, its successor, or the location of its records, can be identified by reference to the BAAF publication *Where to find adoption records: a guide for counsellors* (see Appendix 3 for details).

✓ CHECKLIST 1

Arranging the first interview (England, Wales and Northern Ireland)

1. Receive request for counselling from Registrar General and appoint appropriate counsellor.

2. Send acknowledgement to applicant.

3. Offer appointment. Indicate that:
   - the interview is not a testing situation
   - the applicant will be given their birth name and location
   - they are welcome to bring a 'supporter'
   - they may bring any information they already hold.

4. Note appointment in diary.

5. Ensure an interview room is available.

✓ CHECKLIST 1

Arranging the first interview (Scotland)

1. Receive request for counselling which the adopted person may make by letter, on the telephone or in person.

2. Appoint an appropriate counsellor.

3. Arrange interview. Indicate that the adopted person may bring a supporter and should bring any information they already hold.

4. Note appointment in diary.

5. Ensure an interview room is available.

If you can contact the placement agency before the first interview (or subsequently) you will need to establish:

- the date of any contact between the agency and the birth family
- the reason for the contact
- the action taken by the agency at the time
- any change of name of a birth parent
- the address given by the birth parent or any other member of the birth family
- if any special circumstances were noted concerning health, family, emigration plans, etc.

If the papers to hand or enquiries to the placement agency reveal a family address the counsellor should check the identity of the current residents. This can be done quite simply by telephoning the Electoral Registration Officer at the District Council office covering the address. These enquiries will ensure that the counsellor is forewarned if the applicant for counselling appears keen to trace a parent, as once the applicant has obtained her or his birth certificate checking the address given on the certificate will be the first move. Unfortunately the applicant may check the address by visiting the house!

If it is appropriate to share additional information (other than that contained on the forms supplied by the Registrar General) it can be helpful to both the counsellor and applicant if a typed summary of the key facts is prepared before the interview (see the next section for more guidance on how much and when to share additional information with the applicant). The counsellor can use this as a quick reference whilst talking with the applicant, and then give it to the applicant so that she or he has a tangible record of the details even if all the information was not assimilated at the time. A written summary of information provided will also be helpful at any further sessions and can help reduce the possibility of mis-interpretation or misunderstanding at a later date.

In some cases – for example, if the counselling is being provided by the agency or local authority which arranged the adoption – the counsellor may also have received, or have access to, the agency file. If so, check through it to see if there are any papers, such as letters or photos, which the adopted person may wish to know about and receive at the interview. Such documents can be of great emotional importance to adopted people, and if possible you should photocopy any such documents so that you can keep the photocopy in the file and hand the originals to the adopted person (for further guidance on this, see the section headed *What the counsellor can do* on page 36).

The counsellor in Scotland will not automatically be supplied with any papers or information prior to the first interview. However, it may be that the adopted person in requesting counselling has produced the details they have obtained from the Registrar General or specified their reasons for counselling. In preparing for the interview the counsellor should carefully consider any such information supplied by the adopted person, and check whether any further information or records are immediately available. The Adoption Counselling Centre at Family Care (see Appendix 1 for address) is compiling a computer-based register of adoption orders called the Scottish Adoption Registry which contains sufficient information to identify for adopted people which agency arranged the adoption and where the case records are held. The registry is essentially an administrative service, but is a valuable resource for social workers.

If such information or records are immediately to hand, a summary of the information should be prepared and photocopies taken of any documents that may be given to the adopted person at the interview; if no information or records are immediately available, it is suggested that no further steps be taken until the adopted person has indicated their concerns at the interview.

The first (statutory) interview

There is, of course, no 'statutory interview' as such in Scotland. Adopted people who are given information by the Registrar General may seek counselling or assistance in tracing birth relatives if they wish to do so; details of the entry of birth will usually have been supplied by the time counselling is requested. However, many of the issues outlined below also apply to a 'first interview' provided in Scotland.

Checking proof of identity

During this session the social worker will try to develop a counselling relationship with the adopted person. At the same time key legal requirements must be fulfilled. The first of these – and one frequently overlooked – is a requirement to check the proof of identity brought by the adopted person. The Registrar General's letter to applicants for counselling instructs them to bring along identification, and many individuals think carefully and widely about this. The counsellor should not be cursory when inspecting the identification offered.

The right to birth records information

The statutory requirement to attend an interview equates in most people's minds with a test of suitability (such as, for example, a driving test). Although no mention of being 'approved' or needing to demonstrate a responsible attitude is mentioned in the litera-

✓ CHECKLIST 2

Preparing for the first interview (England, Wales and Northern Ireland)

1. Read carefully the information received from the Registrar General.

2. Are placement records to hand?

   No – go to 3

   Yes – go to 5

3. Try to identify placement agency.

4. Establish availability of any addresses.

5. Check addresses with current register of electors.

6. Prepare summary of information.

7. If agency file already supplied, photocopy documents to give to the adopted person at the interview.

✓ CHECKLIST 2

Preparing for the first interview (Scotland)

1. Read or consider carefully any information supplied by the adopted person and any indication of the reasons they are seeking counselling.

2. Check whether any information or records are immediately available.

   If so:

3. Prepare summary of information.

4. Photocopy documents to give to the adopted person at the interview.

ture available to applicants for birth records information, the compulsory nature of the interview suggests otherwise. It can be reassuring if the counsellor clearly acknowledges at the beginning of the session that the applicant has an unconditional right to the birth certificate information which will be made available during that session.

It is even more helpful if the counsellor stresses the applicant's moral as well as legal right to the information. At the time the provision was introduced in England and Wales the media suggested that whilst seeking out birth parents was now lawful, it remained irresponsible and demonstrated disloyalty to the adoptive family. These overtones still influence many adopted people. A statement of appreciation of the need that many adopted people have to know their background can dispel any doubts and help towards the development of a good counselling relationship.

Some workers have noted that providing the identifying information early in the session reduces tension and reassures the applicant who is then able to concentrate on their discussions with the counsellor – discussions which will now be based on concrete information rather than intangible possibilities. Early provision of birth details will therefore also help to encourage a real counselling relationship.

The adopted person's original name
The importance that is attached to an individual's name is easily overlooked in day-to-day life. It is vital that appropriate importance is attached to the given name and that applicants have time to assimilate and discuss their feelings before moving on to other matters.

Giving further information
Section 51 of the 1976 Adoption Act (which replaced section 26 of the 1975 Children Act on 1 January 1988) gives an adopted adult an absolute right to information that will enable him or her to purchase a copy of his or her original birth certificate. On that basis one could ask 'Why do any more at all?' The statutory responsibility can easily be fulfilled in a single interview. However, the legal entitlement also provides for authority to be given to enable adopted people to ask the court to name the placement agency if possible. This additional provision suggests that it was always the intention of the supporters of this clause that information over and above the birth certificate information should be made available to adopted people.

It may be a salutary exercise for counsellors to ask themselves:
• what do you know of your family's medical history?
• can you identify similarities between your physical appearance and that of your relatives?
• with the assistance of older relatives can you relate details of your birth and your personal history from birth?
• what talents, skills and personality traits run in your family?
• can you understand the rationale behind the important decisions affecting your life, made by adults during your childhood? Have you had the opportunity to question the decision makers?

Once a non-adopted person acknowledges the amount of information available to them and (normally) taken for granted, they can generally begin to understand the difficulties lack of those details can present to an adopted person. Anything that is not readily obtainable soon takes on a disproportionate importance. The counsellor should now appreciate the need, if not the right, to far more information than the basic statutory entitlement.

Nothing will be insignificant to the adopted person. Social workers may find it easier to ask themselves not 'Should I share this information?' but rather 'Do I have a sound reason for not sharing this information?' If the second question is vigorously applied most workers will find it difficult to justify withholding any information at all.

If additional information is available to the social worker at the time of the statutory interview a decision has to be made as to the appropriateness of sharing the extra information with the adopted person at that stage. In deciding whether or not to reveal background information at the statutory interview the counsellor must remember that the first interview is the only certain one. An applicant for counselling who promises to return to discuss the situation before doing anything may leave your office and begin immediate intensive enquiries. The counsellor has to decide whether the risk of the applicant causing distress by acting hastily with limited information is greater than that of a well-informed applicant causing distress by her or his reaction to further information. The counsellor must accept responsibility for information they decide not to reveal as well as for that shared. The social work skill is in quickly assessing applicants and making appropriate judgements as to whether the revelation of a skeleton in the family cupboard would spur them on or hold them back – a difficult but necessary decision.

Great distress has been caused to applicants who find themselves facing a worker armed with a large file to which they have no access. Counsellors should carry into the interview room only those papers that they are willing to show to the applicant.

When working with applicants who claim to want to know only their original name, or just to obtain their original birth certificate, the counsellor should ensure that they are aware that further advice and assistance would be available should they decide to pursue their enquiries at some later stage. Similarly the counsellor should clearly state at the conclusion of the first, and any subsequent, interview either that they have shared all the information that is available on the file or that they have more information that could be shared after further discussions.

Locating the placement agency

If the placement/supervising authority has not been identified already the applicant should be told that the counsellor has a form which may be sent to the court that made the adoption order to authorise the release of information about the agency. Even if the applicant has expressed no interest in making further enquiries the availability of this facility should be explained. If the applicant does not wish to take the court authorisation form at this stage the counsellor can promise to keep it on file so that the applicant may ask for it later should they change their mind.

Information available from the court in Scotland

In Scotland there is no court authorisation form, as adopted people over 17 have the right to read all the papers held by the court in connection with the adoption – the 'court process'. This will include the adoption petition, reports from the curator *ad litem*, the reporting officer and the local authority or adoption society, and any other documents lodged at court in connection with the adoption. The process will have been sealed by the clerk of the court immediately following the adoption, and it must be retained for 100 years. It is held either at the court which dealt with the adoption or at the Scottish Record Office in Edinburgh (sheriff courts send the papers to the Record Office from time to time as their own storage capacity is exhausted – so, for example, the Record Office holds Arbroath records to 1946 only, but has the Edinburgh records to 1965). The adopted person should contact the clerk at the relevant court to check on the location of the process, and they may then arrange to read it.

The Record Office requires the following details to release the process: the adopted person's name at birth; the adoptive parents' names; the name of the sheriff court which granted the adoption order; and the date on which the order was granted. All these details are on the adoption certificate, so the adopted person can if necessary call at New Register House (next door to the Record Office: see Appendix 1 for addresses) to obtain them. There is no fee to see the records held at the Record Office, but no copies are given out: enquirers may sit and read the records in a private room, and take notes. A third party can be nominated to read records if the adopted person is disabled or lives some distance away, although the Record Office encourages people to come themselves where possible. To nominate a third party, the adopted person should write to the Record Office, and give authorisation to the third party, so that the signatures can be compared.

iscussing aims and expectations
Some time in this first session should be used to discuss the applicant's hopes and ideas for moving the enquiry forward. For many people this may have been the first opportunity to dis-

cuss what their adoption means to them. The counsellor may help by suggesting various books from the reading list in Appendix 2 which give practical advice or personal accounts of adoption and reunion experiences.

If the applicant has rigid ideas or obviously unrealistic expectations the counsellor will want to present alternative scenarios, which may be illustrated by careful selection of anecdotal details from the case studies at the beginning of this guide.

Occasionally the counsellor may feel seriously concerned by the aims – either spoken or perceived – of the applicant. If these include reasonable grounds for being concerned for the safety of other individuals the counsellor should consult with his or her line manager and if appropriate take the action outlined in the Department of Health booklet *Access to birth records: notes for counsellors* under the heading 'Difficult situations' ('consider the possibility of contacting other agencies or a doctor or of endeavouring to make contact with the persons [who may be] in danger from the applicant').

If the adopted person wishes to search
If it has been established that the applicant does wish to locate or to contact one or both birth parents – or is considering doing so – the counsellor should offer further opportunities to meet and should explain the assistance that can be offered. This would include the opportunity to discuss the progress of the search, the impact of information gained, and the feelings and responses provoked both in the applicant and within their immediate family; and, on a practical level, inter-agency negotiation, use of reference material and arranging an intermediary.

The importance of using an intermediary discreetly to initiate contact with any traced relatives should be introduced in this session – indeed it is worth mentioning even if the applicant states that she or he has no inclination to locate relatives, as people do change their minds. Similarly, applicants who insist they are 'taking it no further' should be invited to contact the counsellor again if circumstances and intentions change. The aim should be to ensure the message has got across that the door is always open.

Adoption contact registers

The Children Act 1989 included a schedule which amended the 1976 Adoption Act by adding a new section (51A). Under this new section, the Registrar General for England and Wales was empowered to set up an official Adoption Contact Register. The register came into force on 1 May 1991. It is in two parts: Part I for adopted persons, Part II for relatives (meaning any person, other than an adoptive relative, who can prove they are related to the adopted person by blood – including half-blood – or marriage). On payment of a quite substantial fee, the name and address of an adopted person over the age of 18 who wishes to contact any relative of theirs will be entered in Part I. Similarly, the name and address of any relative over the age of 18 who wishes to contact the adopted person will be entered in Part II. If at any time there is a matching registration, the Registrar General will send the name of the relative, and the contact address that they gave, to the adopted person. The relative will be informed this has been done but the adopted person's details are not passed on to the relative, so the responsibility for making contact rests with the adopted person. A registration in either part of the Adoption Contact Register can be cancelled at any time.

If a relative of the adopted person has been entered in Part II of the register, the counsellor will be informed of this by the Registrar General when he supplies the papers for the statutory interview. The counsellor will not be given details of the relative, as these can only be passed on directly to an adopted person who has been registered in Part I. The counsellor will however be able to advise the adopted person that registering will result in being supplied with the name of a relative (not necessarily a parent) and an address through which contact can be made.

If the adopted person wishes to make contact and is not aware of the Adoption Contact Register then they may be advised to register as a first step. To do this they should write to the Registrar General at the General Register Office, Southport (see Appendix 1 for address). The counsellor could also provide one of the free information leaflets about the register available from social services departments or from the Registrar General.

In order to enter their details on the register, adopted people must be able to give the Registrar General their original name, birth mother's name and place of birth – so some people attend a birth records counselling interview if they need to do so to obtain this information. Others will formally apply for birth records counselling to see if additional background information is available. Counsellors will therefore need to establish from their clients whether the present application for birth records counselling is a follow-up step, the applicant having already joined the contact register but not having been advised of a matching registration.

In these cases the adopted person may wish to talk through their feelings about there not being a matching registration. The counsellor should ensure that the adopted person is aware of the wide range of possible reasons why no relative has registered. These may include being unable to afford the registration fee; living abroad or not knowing about the register for other reasons; being unwell; or even having died before the register was established. The fact that a sought relative has not joined this (or any other) contact register is not necessarily an indication of a lack of interest.

In some cases relatives may have misgivings about joining a computerised register operated by a government department, in the mistaken belief that private information about the adoption may become linked to other government computerised records. Others may have reservations about the lack of counselling support afforded by the Adoption Contact Register, and prefer to use the NORCAP or Birth Link registers (see Appendix 1 for addresses) to ensure the involvement of an intermediary. Adopted people should therefore also consider joining one of these registers. In addition these registers may already contain details of the sought relative, as they have been established for several years and have developed into major resources.

The NORCAP register now contains details supplied by over 30,000 individuals, mainly from England and Wales but also from 'ex pats' throughout the world, and matches now occur at almost weekly intervals. Unlike the 'official' Adoption Contact Register, it is possible for people to register notification that contact would be difficult or impossible for them to handle, or to offer only a non-identifying exchange of information via NORCAP. Another major difference is that when a match occurs the co-ordinator writes to both parties to request extra information and informs them of the match within a counselling framework once the match is confirmed. Contact is gradually facilitated at a pace acceptable to both the adopted person and the relative. Registrations are also accepted from adoptive parents of children under 18 years of age and/or in special circumstances (for example, when the adopted person is not able to register for themselves).

The Adoption Counselling Centre in Scotland operates the Birth Link register. This was set up in 1984 following consultations with the Registrar General for Scotland, the Scottish Office, local authority social work departments and voluntary adoption agencies. It allows adopted people, birth parents and birth relatives to register their wish for contact; it also allows birth parents to register their wish not to have contact. In addition, anyone who registers can leave letters, cards or photographs for the person(s) they wish to contact.

Getting hold of the original birth certificate
If the information the counsellor has to hand is limited to the birth certificate information and court authorisation form provided by the Registrar General, the adopted person will need to obtain his or her birth certificate and the information from the court before any further enquiries can be made.

The Registrar General will have provided the birth registration district. If the adopted person sends the form to that local register office, whose address can be obtained from any register office, the certificate will arrive without delay. Postal applications sent to the General Register Office can take up to two months to be processed.

Arranging the next interview

The best suggestion at this stage is for the adopted person to send off for their original birth certificate and apply to the court for identification of the agency. If they telephone the counsellor with the information when the replies are received a further interview can then be arranged.

Having come this far the adopted person may well want to meet again fairly quickly, and the counsellor should try to oblige if the adopted person's need for further discussions seems urgent. However, if the adopted person is prepared to wait a few days longer, the counsellor can then seek to obtain further information from the agency/supervising authority involved in time for the next meeting (for further details on this see the following section on *What the counsellor can do*).

The adopted person should be invited to prepare for the next interview by jotting down everything that he or she can remember ever being told or overhearing about the circumstances of his or her birth or the birth family. It does not matter if it is accurate. There is usually a grain of truth in all rumours and any information may prove useful. The counsellor could casually suggest that the adopted person asks his or her adoptive parents for any details or information that they may have or remember. As well as being a useful source of data this will enable the counsellor to bring the adopters into the dialogue and discuss their attitude, known or assumed, with the adopted person.

✓ CHECKLIST 3

The statutory interview (England, Wales and Northern Ireland)

1. Check identification of applicant.

2. Give applicant form containing their birth records information.

3. Identify agency involved AND/OR offer applicant form to apply to court for this information.

4. Advise applicant you have shared all information available to you OR explain you have further information to hand which you will share after further counselling.

5. Give applicant opportunity to discuss matters relating to his or her adoption, including aims and expectations for moving the enquiry forward.

6. Advise applicant about adoption contact registers.

7. Offer to arrange an intermediary.

8. Invite applicant to further interview.

9. Agree with applicant how/when next session will be arranged.

10. Identify tasks for completion prior to next session.
    Applicant:
    • Apply for original birth certificate.
    • Apply for information from court.
    • Advise counsellor when details available.
    • List everything ever told/heard about birth family.
    Counsellor:
    • Identify current location of records.
    • Request loan of file.
    • Make time and venue available for second session.

11. Return to Registrar General the form showing interview has taken place.

☑ CHECKLIST 3

The first interview (Scotland)

1. Check identification of applicant.

2. Identify agency involved and/or court which made the adoption order. Ensure applicant is aware they are entitled to see the court process.

3. Share any information available to you or explain you have further information to hand which you will share after further counselling.

4. Give applicant opportunity to discuss any matters relating to his or her adoption, including aims and expectations for moving the enquiry forward.

5. Offer to arrange an intermediary.

6. Invite applicant to further interview.

7. Agree with applicant how/when next session will be arranged.

8. Identify tasks for completion prior to next session.
Applicant:
• Arrange to read court process and note details.
• Advise counsellor of relevant details.
• List everything ever told/heard about birth family.
Counsellor:
• Identify current location of agency records.
• Request loan of file.
• Make time and venue available for second session.

Part 4   Searching

The way the search is conducted and the time it may take is infinitely variable. Some people have obtained their original birth certificate at St Catherine's House (the General Register Office) and within a couple of hours have been in possession of the birth mother's present address. Other people have been searching on and off for many years. There is no right or wrong way to search and everyone will have their own ideas, but a systematic search is possible (as outlined later, in the section *How to search*). The counsellor's responsibility is to recommend safe avenues for enquiry which will not cause embarrassment to the person sought. The counsellor will also need to warn against direct approaches to other members of the birth family or the use of enquiry agents inexperienced in adoption, which can often cause distress.

What the counsellor can do

There will be certain information which may not be directly available to the adopted person. If a placement agency is identified the counsellor will need to negotiate the loan of the file or arrange an interview for the adopted person with the placement agency. Information about the circumstances surrounding their adoption will help adopted people appreciate the perspective of the birth parent(s) and develop an understanding of their situation.

If the court records provide an agency name the counsellor can contact it in order to make the checks described on page 27 and also to request the loan of their papers or a comprehensive report to share with the adopted person.

If the court cannot provide an agency name, do not give up. All the addresses given on the original birth certificate should be checked against the list of mother and baby homes contained in *Where to find adoption records* (see Appendix 3). This most useful reference book lists the agencies which used each home, and also provides details of name and location changes over the years, together with details of the holders of records of agencies which are now closed. The book's comprehensive advice on the availability of records can be especially helpful if one encounters an unexpected negative response.

Assistance to unmarried mothers was also provided by many charitable organisations other than adoption agencies. Diocesan and deanery organisations often engaged in 'rescue' and 'moral welfare' work, as did the free churches, convents, etc. Sometimes two or more agencies would co-operate over a placement. One may have comprehensive details of the adopters but scant information on the birth parent(s), whilst at the other the reverse situation might apply. The key to tracing is to keep asking, and if necessary

ain, ask another member of staff,
.e question in a different way or
.t on another day.

aining original documents
Many applicants for birth records counselling will be seeking a tangible link
with their birth family. For some this
may be impossible to achieve because
of difficulties in tracing, the age of the
parents, or their resistance to suggestions of contact. However, many
records do contain these important
links. Photographs may have been left
on file and frequently mothers wrote to
the agency or to their own case worker.

Some agencies have been willing to
provide photocopies of these items for
adopted people, but perhaps the counsellor should ask 'Why should the
adopted person only have a photocopy?' If a copy is legible it will fill the
administrative place in the agency
records, but only the original can fulfil
the emotional needs of the adopted
person. Original letters can be so important to adopted people that it would
be most useful if all agencies could lay
down policies which specify that so
long as agency records are complete,
original documents which originated
from a birth parent should be made
available to a birth records applicant.

With this in mind it is vital that agency
administrators in England and Wales
are made aware that under regulation
14(3) of the Adoption Agencies Regulations 1983 (Circular LAC(84)3) agencies
are instructed that: 'Where a case
record is to be microfilmed and then
destroyed, the agency should first extract any documents which would be
better preserved as originals, such as
photographs or letters from a natural
parent.' (The Scottish regulations [regu-
lation 24(3) of the Adoption Agencies

(Scotland) Regulations 1984] have a
similar provision for microfilming, but
the relevant guidance circular makes
no reference to preserving original documents.)

If a file has been borrowed from another agency and it is found to contain
photographs or letters most adopted
people will greatly appreciate the ef-
forts of their counsellor to advocate on
their behalf in favour of them retaining
the original documents. It is most painful for adopted people to have to accept
that papers of great emotional value to
them have to rest unseen in a locked
repository for administrative reasons.

✓ CHECKLIST 4

What the counsellor can do

1. Obtain adoption file and any extra
   papers from:
   • placement agency
   • supervising authority
   • organisation that assisted birth
   mother
   • any other identified source.

2. Prepare summary for adopted person.

3. Negotiate and agree release of original
   letters and photographs to adopted
   person and replace in file with good
   photocopies.

The second interview
Any interview should begin with an
opportunity for the adopted person to
talk about their thoughts and activities
since the last session. They can be encouraged to do this during the exchange of information that you and
they have uncovered since the first
interview.

The important role for the counsellor is to help the adopted person place any information shared into an appropriate context with regard to social history, social policy, public opinions and media attitudes. The counsellor needs to analyse carefully the judgemental statements and prejudiced remarks which typify old records and to suggest various possible interpretations to the adopted person. (However, before being tempted to develop a superior attitude it may be a little humbling to try to imagine how one's own case recording may read in 30 years time!)

It is likely that in the early stages adopted people will be intent on the searching process and eager for practical advice. Details on how to search, so that counsellors are aware of and can advise on the avenues open to the adopted person, are given in the section on *How to search* (page 41). The adopted person could be advised to get hold of a copy of *Searching for family connections* (see Appendix 2).

Who does what

Adopted people should be encouraged to carry out their searches themselves. By doing so, they retain control over the search, in particular over how far or how quickly they go. The counsellor's role in the search is to give advice and practical help where necessary, and to help the adopted person come to terms with the information they uncover – in other words, to support the adopted person, not to lead them.

The pace at which enquiries progress is infinitely variable. No two searches will be the same and within a single search there will be periods of sudden progress and other times when nothing appears to happen. Whilst there is undoubtedly a value in a counsellor slowing the pace of a very easy and rapid search to allow time for reflection, it is very difficult to find any justification for a counsellor attempting to accelerate an enquiry. A counsellor who is tempted to do so should question whose needs they are trying to meet – their client's or their own. It is most important that the motivation to make and sustain the search stems from the adopted person – not their spouse, nor their children, nor the counsellor. The interest of outside parties in achieving a fairy-tale ending or completing a piece of detective work is irrelevant.

If a social worker controls and/or conducts the search, the adopted person will be under pressure to proceed with direct contact once the birth parent has been located; it will seem an appropriate reward for all the work undertaken. Contact should only be initiated if the adopted person believes it is likely to be right for them and their birth parent, and not for the benefit of any third party.

Sometimes a reduction in the time and energy allocated to the search may be the adopted person's way of withdrawing from something discovered which is unacceptable or disturbing. Some will just need time to digest the information; others may decide not to continue the search.

Applicants for counselling may have strong feelings about all manner of issues such as low-grade occupations, poor housing, criminality, mixed race marriages, or divorce. Whilst a social worker may disapprove of inappropriate and prejudiced value judgements it should be accepted that it would not be in the interests of any party to encourage contact when it is apparent that there are significant differences in personal values.

Adopted people who conduct their own research can withdraw at any stage if they discover any unpalatable information. They do not have to explain or excuse their decision to anyone except themselves.

Locating birth parents

In any search, the aim should always be to locate the birth parent via public records. The purchase of certificates of births, marriages and deaths is expensive, but is essential in order to ensure that the correct person is traced. For searchers in England and Wales, money can be saved by searching the indexes at St Catherine's House and applying for certificates in person. The charge for each certificate ordered in the public search room is less than half the cost charged for postal applications. For searchers in Scotland, the actual entries at New Register House in Edinburgh are available to the public; there are small charges for general searches and for copies of extracts.

A persuasive argument for making effective use of public records is that it serves to protect both the adopted person and the birth parent, as information in the public domain does not involve imagined breaches of confidence or subjective analysis. Similarly, the more information adopted people can obtain the better. Well informed they will be better equipped to make appropriate decisions.

Adopted people should be advised against taking risky short cuts. For example, it may appear much easier to contact a birth mother via her parents who may still live at the birth certificate address. However, unless agency records refer to discussions which included the mother's parents, it is possible they were not aware of their daughter's pregnancy. To protect the birth mother's privacy and confidentiality she should be contacted direct and not via her parents or other relatives or colleagues.

Even if one can be sure that the parents were aware of the birth it may still be advisable not to direct an approach to the birth mother via her parents. They will inevitably remember the great distress of their daughter when she parted with her child; they may wish to avoid reopening old wounds and deny that their daughter would want to have contact with the adopted person. They may be protective of their daughter's marriage and their grandchildren and therefore also decline all contact. These decisions may well be taken without reference to their daughter. Her views may be entirely different to those of her parents, or they may simply have misjudged her likely reaction. If the grandparents do make an inappropriate response it could lead to years of distress for both the adopted person and the birth mother; and any later contact could cause hostile repercussions between the mother and her parents.

Advice on direct contact

Many applicants for birth records counselling who go on to search will eventually locate the current address of their birth parent. Despite earlier assurances that they would consult the counsellor before approaching a found parent, a number will initiate direct contact as soon as an address is to hand. In some cases the approach will be welcomed, but the counsellor will probably never know, as in such cases applicants tend to get in touch only if they need the counsellor's help to resolve difficulties.

If at the end of the second interview

you do not make a firm appointment for another meeting with the applicant, it is worth stressing that you are available at all times if they should need advice or be uncertain about how to proceed. It is also worth reiterating that the use of an intermediary to initiate contact once the birth parent has been located can help reduce the stress that both the adopted person and the birth parent are likely to feel.

If a birth parent has died

Adopted people who begin searching whilst under 40 will probably expect to find their birth parent alive, and hopefully in good health. Unfortunately this will not always be the case, and the counsellor should try to prepare the adopted person for the possibility of discovering that the parent has already died. The counsellor should also be aware of the complex emotional difficulties which may arise in such a situation.

In a few cases the counsellor may have the information on file – for example, if the mother had died in childbirth. It is also possible that the information from the Registrar General may include a letter indicating that the parent was suffering from a terminal illness, in which case the counsellor should make careful enquiries to establish the present position in order to be able to pass on any information as sensitively as possible.

The death of a sought parent is a possibility when adopted people who check the electoral registers find family members at the parent's last known address, but not the parent. If a spouse is still living at the address then a divorce or death are the two most likely reasons for the absence of the sought parent. Both possibilities can be easily checked using public records – in England and Wales, the indexes of deaths at St Catherine's House or the divorce records at Somerset House (see Appendix 1 for addresses; the indexes of deaths are the easiest to access).

If it is found that the birth parent has died, handling this knowledge may prove very difficult. Although the adopted person will not have 'known' the birth parent, they may still be overwhelmed by grief: the parent has been lost to the adopted person and they can feel as bereaved as any other person whose parent has died. The bereavement will be harder to bear if the adopted person's own family and friends are unable to accept this reaction as normal.

If the parent died prematurely or in tragic circumstances the adopted person may also suddenly become aware of their own mortality – particularly if the parent died at a similar age to that of the adopted person when he or she learns of the death. The adopted person may also feel a responsibility for the parent's death. They may feel that if they had searched and made contact with the parent earlier the death could have been avoided, especially if depression or loneliness appear to have been contributory factors.

Adopted people in this situation will be helped by bereavement counselling to acknowledge that the grief that they feel is normal. Practical steps such as visiting the grave or crematorium memorial may help. The counsellor might attempt to make contact with surviving relatives, who may feel able to meet the adopted person and share knowledge of the parent. If a personal momento or keepsake can be provided this can be very helpful.

The second interview

1. Has enough time been given to talking things through?

2. Discuss acceptable/risky methods of searching.

3. Provide advice/guidelines on searching; suggest purchase of *Searching for family connections.*

4. Recommend that adopted person works quite slowly so as to have time to absorb and think over each discovery made.

5. Discuss the possibility that the birth parent may have died.

6. Stress that you are available for advice/further meetings as the search progresses.

7. Give further reminder of the need for an intermediary.

How to search

This section has been adapted with kind permission from *Searching for family connections* published by NOR-CAP (see Appendix 2 for details).

The two main avenues to search are the electoral registers and the records at the General Register Office.

The electoral registers

These can show at once if the address on the birth certificate was that of the mother's family home. Contact the Electoral Registration Officer for the town shown as the mother's home, and find out where the Register of Electors for the year of the adopted person's birth can be seen (eg at the district council offices or the county record office; by prior arrangement it can also be seen at the British Library in London). If a visit is not possible, the adopted person should write and ask who is listed at the address given on the birth certificate. The registers are compiled each autumn and are effective from the following February, so it would be best to check the register each side of the date of birth. Even if members of the mother's family are listed, the mother's name may not appear as only those over the age of 20 are shown before 1965, and those over 17 from 1966.

If it is established that this was the family home, the adopted person should check forward year by year and note all the names listed. The mother may appear in a later year with a 'Y' against her name. The date of this entry should be noted, as the 'Y' indicates that she was between 20 and 21 in that year – useful information if it is necessary to obtain a copy of her birth certificate later.

If the whole family disappears from the register, it probably means they moved house. Individual members dropping off could suggest children growing up and leaving home to work elsewhere, or more likely to marry. It may be found that the mother married and lived with her husband in her parents' home for one or more years. It can also be useful to make a note of the names of any long-term neighbours. It may well help to visit the road. If it is obviously council housing, or has been redeveloped, the district council may be able to help with information from their rehousing records.

If, having worked forward to the present day, the adopted person finds that there are still relatives of the mother living at the original address, or that some old neighbours are still in the area, it may be a good time to make some enquiries using a story which is as near to the truth as possible without arousing suspicions among neighbours, friends or relatives of the mother. The same story should be used with each person asked, in case they talk about it among themselves. If possible the adopted person should make these enquiries by telephone or letter, as there is a slight chance that facial similarities will give the secret away. The story should be practised until it can be told convincingly and without hesitation, but it should not sound rehearsed.

An acceptable story could be: My mother (ie the adoptive mother) was good friends with (name of mother from birth certificate; they probably never met, but no doubt the mother sees the woman who gave her a child as a friend). This was back in the (take from date of birth, but do not be too precise, eg early fifties) when (first name of birth mother) was working as (information from occupation given on birth certificate, but again do not be too precise, eg a machinist). We found, when having a clear-out recently, that we had some photographs we think she would like (she is almost certain to be interested in pictures of her child) and we wondered if you could tell us if she is married and where she lives now.

If the mother's whereabouts have not yet been found, then it may be time to try the other main search avenue: the General Register Office.

The General Register Office

The adopted person should begin by trying to find an entry for the mother's marriage. Marriages are indexed in alphabetical order and bound in volumes, one for each quarter of each year.

The search should start from the last known date that the mother was still single (this could be the date of the adopted person's birth), or the year in which the mother last appeared on the electoral roll under her maiden name. When this entry is found, the adopted person should apply for the full marriage certificate. Although quite expensive, it is a good investment as it will state not only the full names of the mother and her husband, but also their ages, occupations and addresses at the time of marriage. This provides another useful address to check with the electoral register.

Once evidence has been found of the mother's marriage, the adopted person should start looking for births of children. The search should begin in the same quarter as that in which the marriage was found. Unless the adopted person is trying to build up a complete picture of the mother's family, it is not necessary to buy a copy of the full certificate for each child born. The searcher should simply make a note of the reference number and continue searching until it would seem they have found the record for the youngest child. By now they may be almost up to date, so they should obtain a copy of the full birth certificate of the youngest child. This may give yet another address to check with the electoral register.

If all or any of the mother's other children are over 16, the marriage registers can be checked and, once again, the most recent certificate obtained, which could give the mother's present address. If the adopted person finds details of the marriage of half-brothers or -sisters, a visit to the public library near their home to see old copies of local newspapers might be helpful – a picture and report of the wedding could considerably increase knowledge of the family.

When searching the indexes at St Catherine's House, the adopted person may be uncertain as to whether an entry found is the correct one. A leaflet is available from the cashier explaining the reference checking system. Basically, the adopted person applies for the certificate and lists on the back of the application what they know would be the correct details if this was the entry they were looking for (eg the full name of the mother). If the details do not agree with the registered details, the adopted person receives a refund of half the fee (instead of a certificate which would be useless to them). There is a similar reference checking system when looking for a marriage certificate for which the adopted person has found several possible entries.

The Scottish system is more straightforward in that the actual entries at New Register House are available to the public. Therefore full details from, for example, a marriage certificate, can be obtained at the time of a search – making it easier to avoid following up the wrong person.

Both NORCAP and the Adoption Counselling Centre (Family Care) undertake searches on behalf of adopted people who are unable to do so themselves; a fee is charged for this service.

Other public or official records
If it is suspected that the mother's marriage may have ended in divorce, the adopted person should call at Somerset House in London where the clerk on duty will search the microfilmed records. If the search is successful, a copy of the divorce record can be ob-

tained. This will give the names of the petitioner, respondent, and in some cases co-respondent (which can be a useful clue when looking for a subsequent remarriage: in the St Catherine's House register the bride would be entered under her previous married name). The adopted person could also check the probate register at Somerset House to see if the grandparents left a will: this may give the name and address of the family solicitor who may be able to help.

In Scotland, marriage records are held by the Registrar General at New Register House; these will indicate whether a marriage has ended in divorce. If the adopted person wishes to see the court records relating to the divorce process, they should contact the Scottish Record Office to enquire as to the whereabouts of the records, which will depend upon the date of the divorce.

The most serious difficulty the adopted person is likely to encounter is if the mother decided to live with someone as a common law wife. If she used her partner's surname and any children were registered under his name, she would be very difficult to trace.

If the address on the adopted person's birth certificate was not the mother's family home, then the search will be more difficult. If an entry cannot be found for the mother's marriage in the indexes, it may be worth trying to obtain a copy of her birth certificate. The agency which arranged the adoption should have a record of how old the mother was when the adopted person was born, so the approximate date of the mother's birth can be worked out.

The placing agency could also be asked if they have a note of the then family address. If this address was given to them in confidence they may be unwilling to divulge it, but one of their social workers could make careful enquiries on the adopted person's behalf.

Telephone directories are a useful way of checking entries from birth and marriage certificates which are a few years out of date – remember, however, that not everyone has a telephone, and some who do are ex-directory. It is probably best to use telephone directories to exclude negative results from the list of possible addresses rather than as a means of positive identification.

Other possible avenues to try include Kelly's street directories; *Who's who* in case the adopted person has a famous relative; or the professional lists if the mother was, or was married to, a solicitor, barrister, accountant, doctor, nurse or clergyman.

In any case it is essential to double-check all information: eg if the mother is traced through the electoral rolls, the confirming entries should be checked in the indexes at the General Register Office. Similarly, if the search is unsuccessful, it may be that a vital entry has been missed; it may be worth repeating the search.

Other methods
(Note that these approaches would have to be handled very carefully; see the section below on *Using methods other than public records* for more advice.)

Radio presenters might be persuaded to broadcast the adopted person's story on a suitable programme: even if the mother does not hear the item, someone who knows her may write in. The letters page of a woman's magazine or local newspaper could also be tried.

A carefully worded advertisement could be placed in the personal column of a national or local newspaper. If the adopted person can afford it, a solicitor might be asked to place one on their behalf: solicitors' requests for someone to contact them always make people think of money or an unexpected inheritance!

An attempt could be made to trace one of the mother's sisters, brothers or maybe children. This could be a useful idea if the mother's married name was very common while one of her sisters had married someone with an unusual surname.

Using methods other than public records
Most determined searchers will succeed in locating birth relatives but for a small group every line of enquiry will lead to a brick wall. This may be because the parent gave false information at the time of the adoption, or because she or he lives an isolated or very unconventional life.

When all the 'safe' methods have been exhausted the adopted person may be tempted to take risks. The counsellor will probably share the adopted person's frustration and should avoid being judgemental. Previously rejected methods could now be examined, but the risks to both the adopted person and the birth relatives would need to be carefully evaluated.

The counsellor may not like the idea of resorting to such 'risky' techniques, but if the adopted person is determined she or he will go ahead with or without the counsellor's approval, so on balance it is probably best to be supportive and stay involved. You can never tell when the counsellor's help may be needed.

What to do when the search is successful

Many adopted people will seek the assistance of their counsellor once they have located their birth parent: they recognise the profound significance of the task they are taking on and of the information they now hold, and welcome the opportunity to explore its potential impact on themselves and both their birth and immediate families.

Whilst wishing to proceed as quickly as possible it is important that adequate preparation is undertaken. At this stage – more so than at the initial interview, or even at those interviews relating to the searching process – a really useful counselling relationship can be developed.

The counsellor must first double-check the adopted person's research. Play devil's advocate; question all assumptions. If you are being asked to initiate contact you need to be absolutely sure you will be approaching the correct person. There should be no unexplained gaps in the line of research.

The adopted person's aims and expectations

The information that the adopted person is likely to have obtained will include basic factual details about the birth parent's occupation, home location and family background – in other words, details about the parent's life since the adoption was arranged, such as if, when and to whom they were married. The adopted person will also have arrived at a more subjective analysis of such things as the known or assumed reasons for the adoption, the

✓ CHECKLIST 6

What to do when the search is successful

1. Talk through searching methods and results.

2. Acknowledge impact of information gained.

3. Carefully check research. Has correct person been found?

4. What assumptions are being made about the circumstances of the adoption, the birth mother, etc?

5. Identify adopted person's current aims and objectives.

length of time between the adoption and first or subsequent marriage, whether or not the marriage was to the other parent, and the names given to any further children.

The adopted person's feelings about this information, and about what they hope will result from making contact, will need to be carefully discussed. For example, adopted people may at this stage present as wanting only details of the circumstances surrounding their birth. However, most will admit to hoping for at least one meeting, and secretly many would like an ongoing relationship to result. For those who grew up as only children there is frequently a hope that they may establish contact with a brother or sister, and so make up for the lack of sibling relationships in childhood. This in particular is an area which will need careful examination, as real sibling relationships result from shared childhood experience; nevertheless, close special friendships can develop.

One way of helping the adopted person to prioritise their aims is to ask them to verbalise their ideal outcome, prompted perhaps by the idea of the counsellor being able to wave a magic wand and fulfil all their wishes (this must, of course, be balanced by reality). The adopted person could then be asked which of all their wishes or dreams is the one which matters most. They should also be encouraged to work out what is the least they hope to learn or gain from making contact (such as a photograph, medical information, the name of the other parent, or the reason for the adoption). Armed with this information a skilled intermediary should then be able to achieve at least one key objective as a result of the contact except in the most hostile situations.

The next section of this book looks in detail at the areas to be explored before contact is made; how to choose an intermediary; and how to make contact and arrange a meeting.

Areas to be explored prior to initiating contact

The adopted person's responsibilities
An adopted person has an absolute right to their birth records. As in many areas of life, along with rights come responsibilities. As the instigator of the contact the adopted person must accept responsibility for it.

Not only should they be mindful of the parent's right to privacy – secrecy even if that is their choice – but they should appreciate that, although their own attitudes and feelings may be paramount before any contact is made, once an approach has been made the other party's feelings must be taken into account. The actions of the adopted person may have serious consequences for the birth parent, so every move must allow for their feelings as well as the needs of the adopted person.

The counsellor or intermediary must ensure that the adopted person is sufficiently prepared to follow through any contact. Once the contact has been made there can be no going back. The elegant lady spotted leaving the large Victorian house may not be the birth mother, who could be frail and bedridden in one of the many bedsits into which the house is divided. The parent could be lonely, isolated, embittered. The moment contact is established the parent may see this as the opportunity to realise their hopes and an end to their personal tragedy: they assume that this long lost child will now provide all the affection and comfort missing from their life. The adopted person must be prepared to deal with such a response, even if it may not be quite what they expected.

There will inevitably be occasional cases where the birth parent may feel that the daughter or son they gave up for adoption has benefited from their sacrifice – and at the cost of their unhappiness. Such a parent may expect the adopted person to compensate them, and such pressure will be difficult to escape emotionally even if any financial claims are easily withstood.

Consideration of who knows about the adoption
The only person who it is safe to assume knows about the existence of the adopted person is the birth mother. One can only assume her parents were aware if they were specifically mentioned or interviewed in connection with the adoption, and this has been confirmed by reference to the placement agency's records. It is best to be over-cautious: assume people do not know until you have firm evidence that they do.

A birth mother's husband (if he is not also the birth father) is more likely to know of her pregnancy if he was living in the same area or if they were in contact very soon after the birth. The experience of NORCAP suggests that the vast majority of husbands of birth mothers are aware of the child placed for adoption, but that this is frequently a taboo subject, one which may not have been mentioned since the marriage.

Knowledge of the child placed for adoption does not appear to hold true for subsequent children, as understandably many parents find it impossible to explain to young children that they have an 'unseen' elder brother or sister; and once the children are older and better able to understand about adoption, telling them of their half-sibling becomes even more difficult, as the inevitable question is 'Why didn't you tell me before?'

Fear of who may need to be told of the adoption, or who may find out about their past, is the most frequent reason for a birth parent initially declining contact.

Comparing lifestyles

Lois Rayner in her study *The adopted child comes of age* (George Allen & Unwin, 1980) suggested that adoption conferred upward social mobility. In many cases, particularly for placements made between 1945 and 1965, this will indeed be the case. Much will depend on the adopted person's upbringing as to how well they cope with any differences between their own lifestyle and that of the birth family. The style of house and standard of housekeeping are far more important to some people than to others. Names of meals can lead to misunderstanding: if invited to dinner, will someone arrive at 11.30am or 8.00pm? If asked to tea, will they expect cucumber sandwiches at four or a three-course meal at six? Such differ-

ences, though superficial, can make people feel uncomfortable and therefore hinder the development of any relationship. It is best if these points can be discreetly checked out in advance before they cause any embarrassment.

The church may be an important factor in the life of one family but irrelevant to the other; one family may try to convert the other and in so doing cause resentment. Financial background should also not be overlooked. Is the adopted person looking for 'compensation'? This will be a question raised in the mind of at least one member of the birth family even if it is not put into words. Alternatively, will the birth family expect a well-off 'child from the past' to support them? Common questions include 'is she (or he) a bit stuck up?' or 'will they mind, we're only ordinary?', so there will be many fears to be allayed.

Transracial adoptions

In some cases it will be necessary to help the adopted person consider racial or cultural differences. In cases of transracial adoption it is important that a skilled black worker is available to offer appropriate help and support. If there is no black worker available within the agency offering the counselling, then assistance should be sought from specialist agencies (both BAAF and specialist agencies like the Post-Adoption Centre have black workers who can provide this support – see Appendix 1 for addresses).

A black person who has been transracially adopted may have been helped by their white adoptive family to develop a positive black identity, but in some cases they will have had little contact with black people, no knowledge of their own culture, and be very unsure of their own racial identity. Their adoptive experience can raise important issues both for the adopted person and for the birth family – for example, as the Post-Adoption Centre's paper *A glimpse through the looking glass** indicates, adopted people may have a strong desire to share the 'hurt and pain and confusion they experienced whilst growing up in [an] adoptive family', while the birth family may be unaware of or not fully appreciate 'the cultural vacuum the adopted people feel they have inhabited throughout their life'. Transracially adopted people may welcome the opportunity to read *A glimpse through the looking glass* and to discuss it with the counsellor. The awareness that other people have had similar experiences will help to normalise the situation they have experienced and to overcome feelings of isolation.

The counsellor should ensure that wherever possible they have accurate cultural background information about each birth parent, as this is a key factor in an adopted person's identity. Special care will be needed where the adopted person is of mixed parentage. The counsellor and the adopted person will need to consider the possible effect of any prevailing social attitudes at the time of the adoption, as these may have contributed to the birth parent's decision to give up the child, and may have implications for how the birth parent would respond to renewed contact with their son or daughter.

A black person who has been adopted by white parents may be particularly

anxious to establish contact with their black birth parent. In many cases the black parent will be the father, and often the only means of obtaining information about a birth father is to ask the birth mother. Where the parents are of different racial background this can be a most sensitive issue, and the adopted person may even face overt or covert racism when an approach is made to the birth family. Once again this is an area in which advice from black specialists will prove invaluable.

Involvement with the birth family
The adopted person must appreciate that their arrival may have a considerable impact on the birth family. The level of acceptance they can expect and the speed with which it can be achieved will depend to a large extent on how much was known about the adoption prior to the contact being initiated. If everyone in the birth parent's present family is aware of the adoption then the feelings of the family may well mirror those of the parent.

In such cases, where nothing is kept secret and where the adopted person is given a warm welcome, it is easy to be led into believing that a problem-free reunion has been achieved. The euphoria is unlikely to last. As with a new baby that is the focus of attention, it is not long before a sibling or a spouse begins to feel left out and displays signs of jealousy or insecurity.

When an initial meeting has gone well everyone will be keen to see close ties develop. This provides assurance for all parties that making contact was the right thing to do. However, everyone must appreciate that the new relationship cannot ever be the same as one that is based on shared family life right through childhood. The experience of

---

Shekleton J *A glimpse through the looking glass* Post-Adoption Centre Discussion Paper no 8, September 1990.

NORCAP intermediaries suggests that the fundamental basis of such new relationships must be carefully reviewed.

For most of the population affection between parent and child and between siblings is channelled throughout its development by accepted restraints on sexual behaviour. The incest taboo surrounds and pervades most family life, and with the exception of abused children few individuals ever need to consider that laws relating to incest even exist, let alone consider the consequences of transgressing such laws. However, when a new family member is encountered the position is different. These people are linked by close kinship, and society expects them to feel affection for each other; but there are few guidelines defining the love between mother and son, father and daughter, brother and sister which is not born of shared lives, experience, and intimate caring.

Adding to this confusion is the possibility that for the adopted person this may be their first contact with someone to whom they are genetically related. Anthropologists and psychologists are currently engaged in research into genetic sexual attraction. In all species attraction exists between those who are quite similar, and it is now believed that the attraction that would otherwise exist between close family members is muted by the shared care and nurturing experiences which are typical of family life. This perhaps explains why adopted people do not appear to be sexually attracted to members of their adoptive family (although, with the exception of the adoptive parents, such a relationship would be legally acceptable).

Most reunions will not develop into these problem areas, but it is important that these issues are looked at in every preparation. The adopted person, and subsequently the birth family members, will probably dismiss the suggestion out of hand and reaffirm the strength of their existing relationships. However, once the topic has been raised, in the few cases where difficulties do arise the adopted person will be able to approach their counsellor knowing that the situation is not unique, and they are not abnormal or deviant. The earlier discussion in hypothetical terms makes it possible for the adopted person or any birth family member to ask for help and support.

Counsellors and intermediaries should be aware that some situations can be at greater risk of misplaced sexual feelings than others. These include contact between full and half siblings who have no previous experience of sibling relationships, and situations where a female adopted person seeking contact with her birth father is of similar age to (and closely resembles the appearance of) her mother at the time of the relationship between the parents. Similarly at risk are situations where a male adopted person reminds his birth mother of his father. In these cases the attraction may not be between parent and child so much as an opportunity for the parent to relive a previous relationship. Parents may be particularly vulnerable to such confusion if they are already experiencing some mid-life difficulties and insecurity.

It has also recently been noted that some young male adopted people may attempt to use a sexual relationship to demonstrate the power that they hold over their found birth mother. Specialist advice should be sought (eg from the Post-Adoption Centre) if the counsellor fears for the well being of the mother. Fortunately such cases are very rare but those which do develop can have dire consequences, and the counsellor should not be inhibited by a sense of disbelief from seeking experienced help.

The attitude of the adopted person's immediate family

Adopted people will frequently assure the counsellor that their partner, and children, fully support their actions. It is vital to examine this claim closely as the adopted person is likely to need all available support, regardless of the outcome, and a partner nursing secret hostility will not be able to provide this unconditional support. It must also be established who is the real instigator of the enquiry. Partners can encourage adopted people to make contact to fulfil their own day-dreams or to satisfy curiosity, and neither is an appropriate reason for initiating contact.

Partners are often closely involved in the research. They may even undertake most of the leg work and be the one to discover the parent's address. Having been so involved it can be difficult to take a back seat, but at the point of contact the birth parent is going to be interested in their son or daughter, and not – at least at first – in the spouse or children. In fact to admit such people exist can be painful, for it involves acknowledging that their 'child' is now an adult, in many ways a stranger, with a life of their own; and acknowledging this requires immediate acceptance of the many missing years.

If the adopted person agrees, it can be useful to have at least one preparatory session with the whole family. The demands of any new relationship may be such as temporarily to jeopardise existing relationships. Searching for, and reunion with, birth parents is an emotional, stressful and potentially traumatic experience. All the family will be affected by the contact and some may be left feeling that it has had a derogatory impact on them. It should therefore be pointed out that many happy reunions are followed by a 'honeymoon' period when the whole of the adopted person's attention will be focused on the found parent: existing relationships may seem insignificant, and everyone else apart from the found parent will be treated in an off-hand manner. This can be very hurtful, especially for a partner who undertook much of the search. It will help if everyone is aware that no honeymoon lasts for ever: eventually there will be a disagreement and a more realistic perspective will emerge.

A family meeting will also give the counsellor the chance to weigh up the family dynamics and to establish the real instigator of the contact. It should be possible to work out if the search has been prompted by a need for affection and if the partner has the personal resources to support the adopted person as expected. Having had direct contact with the counsellor, the other family members will also then feel able to seek help themselves should the need arise in the future.

The adoptive parents

It may be that the adoptive parents are included in the family session, in which case their views will be known to the counsellor. If they are never mentioned the counsellor, taking care not to suggest any censure of the adopted person, must include them in the topics discussed.

Many adopted people harbour secret

guilt that contact with their birth family reflects badly on their adopters or demonstrates disloyalty, and this is often the reason for attempts to keep the contact a secret. The counsellor can help by clearly acknowledging the adopted person's right to know and emphasising the normality of the exercise.

It is important to check out both practical and emotional issues. Does the adopted person and her or his family have frequent contact with the adoptive parents? Do they live locally? Do they read each other's greetings cards on birthdays and at Christmas? Are the adoptive parents used as babysitters or daytime childminders? If there are many positive answers to these questions the adopted person should be warned of the practical difficulties of keeping any ongoing contact secret. It will put them under stress and necessitate encouraging their children to be untruthful. Do they want to find themselves in a situation where they are saying to their child 'Don't tell Grandma where we went yesterday'? If adopted people do not wish to introduce a plethora of white lies into their children's lives they might be open to the suggestion that their adoptive parents may be more hurt by being excluded than by knowledge of their adopted daughter or son's need to search.

It might help here to discuss how the adopted person first learned they were adopted. If they were kindly and appropriately told they may be able to acknowledge that the adoptive parents probably found it difficult and frightening to have to impart that knowledge and were themselves fearful that their child would reject them or feel unloved. The adopted person will appreciate how much easier it may have

seemed for the adoptive parents to decide not to tell, avoid the risk of any upset, and let their adopted daughter or son find out themselves at some later stage. But how would the adopted person have felt if they had found out from a schoolfriend, or from family documents? From this perspective an adopted person should appreciate the risk of ultimately causing greater distress to their adoptive parents by not telling them now, and then seeing them find out later from a third party.

✓ CHECKLIST 7

Areas to be explored prior to initiating contact

1. Adopted person's responsibilities as a result of initiating contact.

2. Identifying who will know about the adoption.

3. Comparison of adopted person's and birth family's lifestyles.

4. Discussion of racial and cultural issues in transracial adoptions.

5. Coping with likely impact on the birth family.

6. Risks of relationship developing sexually.

7. Meeting with adopted person's own family.

8. Position with regard to adoptive parents.

Choosing an intermediary

The adopted person may ask the counsellor to act as intermediary. Whilst the counsellor is best placed to prepare the adopted person for contact, they should carefully consider whether they or some other individual will make the most suitable intermediary.

The adopted person, their partner or close friend should be immediately excluded as the person who should make the initial contact with the birth parent: none of them could objectively appreciate the feelings of the birth parent.

If one considers the air of secrecy that used to surround adoption – and that may well still persist from the birth parent's perspective – the need for discretion is obvious. Can any individual who was involved in the original placement be located? If no caseworker is available perhaps the agency is still operational? Using such an intermediary can protect birth parents from fears that their secret has been revealed to every Tom, Dick and Harriet. If the counsellor's agency was not the one originally involved this may require the negotiation of a piece of joint work.

In some circumstances it may be necessary to be a little cautious of using record-holding agencies. For example, the records of the large National Children's Adoption Agency – the 'Knightsbridge Agency' – are now held by Westminster Social Services Department. Departments such as this are under intense inner-city pressures and it is unreasonable to expect them to allocate valuable staff time to an area of work arising from a primarily archivist role. The advantage of the parent being able to identify with the instigator of the contact is in any case lost in such circumstances. (In contrast, Family Care in Edinburgh holds records other than its own – it acts as agent for Lothian Region in respect of the Church of Scotland records and the Episcopalian records – yet the above reservations

would not apply, as Family Care offers a specialist intermediary service.)

If there is no obvious past link available the counsellor has to identify an intermediary from a limited list, each possible choice having its own advantages and disadvantages, as set out in the chart on pages 54-55.

Whoever acts as intermediary the counsellor's role as supporter and adviser to the adopted person continues. If someone else is entrusted with the intermediary role the adopted person might need to lean on their own counsellor in the tense period whilst awaiting a response from the birth relative.

Obviously, in situations where the counsellor does not her- or himself act as the intermediary, the intermediary will need to be fully briefed on the circumstances of the adoption and the wishes of the adopted person.

How to make contact

There are really only three options: to visit, to telephone, or to write a letter.

Visiting has few advantages apart from seeing the person face to face, and is potentially risky. Although as intermediary you may have considerable factual knowledge of the person you wish to approach, you will have very little information about their day-to-day life. You have no idea who may answer the door, who else may be at home, who may overhear what you say; neither do you have any clue as to what may be happening in that household on the day you call – a party, a funeral, an argument, a court appearance. An unexpected visit from any official in such circumstances would be unwelcome and, given the sensitive nature of your errand, predisposes it to failure.

Choosing an intermediary

	Advantages
The birth records counsellor	• The counsellor has done all the preliminary work, understands the adopted person's perspective and feels able to accurately represent him or her
Social services/social work department for the area covering the birth parents' home	• Local help is available to the parent • A letter can be explained as a routine enquiry from 'the Council' • The intermediary may be aware of any major home pressures on the birth family
Specialist counselling agency (eg NORCAP)	• Personal service and extended availability (eg direct access to intermediary for the birth parent rather than through a receptionist) may make it easier for the parent to respond • Natural extension of work done with applicant if s/he has had previous contact with the specialist counselling agency • NORCAP intermediary will be as local as possible to birth relative
Staff member of original placement agency	• May know something of relative's current situation and also be aware who in family knows about the adoption • Could possibly be the same worker involved at the time of the adoption, whose name the relative would recognise (would avoid the need for explanation in letter) • Relative does not have to fear breach of confidentiality
Member of clergy or religious order	• Acceptable 'unexpected' caller to some people • May be neutral and non-judgemental • May be identified as suitable figure already known to relative

Disadvantages

- Questions may arise when a letter is received from an agency in another part of the country. Family members may demand an explanation
- The intermediary may be a long way from the parent if they request a personal meeting to discuss the situation

- The counsellor and adopted person have assumed they can trust the department to act appropriately. The birth parent may be in dispute with the department and not share that trust
- The parent may be known to the department in another capacity – eg as a client or a social worker – and may resent this other facet of their life being disclosed to the department

- May be inappropriate if this is adopted person's first contact with agency (intermediary service at NORCAP is based upon befriending of the adopted person by the NORCAP volunteer)
- Intermediary may not be local to the adopted person

- Relative may be hostile to agency or key worker; may not welcome new contact with professional who remembers her/him when very vulnerable and powerless
- Relative may assume letter to be standard follow-up and not appreciate its personal nature; adopted person may therefore wait longer for a response

- May not possess counselling skills
- May not appreciate fully the dynamics of reunion situations
- Relative may resent this involvement

Telephoning carries similar risks (and in any case not everyone has a telephone). As you do not see the person to whom you are speaking the opportunity for revealing all to the wrong person is increased: for example, there could well be two Mrs Mary Jones living in the same house, one being the daughter-in-law of the person you intended to speak with. Also, many people use the telephone out of necessity only, and are not at all happy when required to engage in emotional and personal conversations. There is the additional risk that the information given may not be taken in at once, and the parent may make a hasty response without the benefit of time for reflection.

Writing a letter is therefore the least hazardous alternative. There is the possible risk that the recipient will be unable to read, but most people in such a predicament will have developed coping strategies for dealing with forms and letters. The important skill is to balance the content of the letter so that the intended recipient will grasp its purpose but any other person who reads it will be unable to guess the nature of the enquiry (unless the birth parent has made them fully aware of the situation).

John Stroud, the Assistant Director of Hertfordshire Social Services Department until shortly before his death in 1989, was highly experienced in this area of work. He used a simple, standard form of words which met the above criteria:

I wonder if you can help and advise me with an enquiry I have had from a young woman who was born in (date) in (place). She thinks she is connected to the .... family. I do realise this is quite a common name, but if you think this may be your branch of the family, please drop me a note and I will be happy to pursue it.

Obviously this form of words will need to be adapted according to the circumstances – for example, if the family name is particularly unusual, the last sentence should be adapted to something like: 'I do realise that this may not be your branch of the family, but if you think that it might be, please drop me a note ... etc.'

When signing the letter, use a non-specific designation such as 'Social worker' rather than, for example, 'Adoption officer'. Similarly, be careful not to use headed paper which says, for example, 'Adoption and Fostering Team'.

In sending such a letter one should try to envisage the 'breakfast cereal advertisement' family (the family where everyone sits around the table together for a leisurely meal – imagine your letter arriving for the mother in the middle of breakfast) or a 'Victorian' style family where the male head of the household reads all incoming mail before distributing it to the intended recipient. There is nothing in the letter above which would reveal any secret the mother has kept. If she is agitated by its arrival an obvious excuse is built into the letter. If she needs to make the gesture she can throw the letter away: she can always recover it later. It demands no immediate action and can be dealt with when she chooses, from home, from work or from a trusted friend's address. The recipient now holds the initiative and perhaps at this stage it is her (or his) right to do so.

Intermediaries should not send off a letter or otherwise initiate contact at a time when they would not be able to immediately deal with any response (eg if they were about to go on annual leave).

✓ CHECKLIST 8

How to make contact

1. Decide method in light of circumstances.

2. Keep letter simple; don't inadvertently give away the letter's purpose in the designation or letterhead.

3. Ensure that other commitments will not unduly delay dealing with any response.

The birth parent's feelings

The counsellor should ensure that the adopted person is aware of the possible reactions that the approach may provoke and of the likely feelings of the birth parent. Intermediaries also need to be sensitive to these issues, as they will be the initial point of contact for the birth parent. She (or he) is likely to be experiencing a rapidly changing mixture of emotions, and may well herself (or himself) be seeking advice or reassurance before agreeing to further contact. The intermediary should be able to advise on any immediate concerns, but if the birth parent requires individual counselling this should be arranged for them either through the intermediary's own agency or through a specialist agency (see Appendix 1 for addresses).

The birth parent's reactions can range from an unconditional enthusiastic welcome to prolonged silence or even hostility. In England and Wales, the birth parent may have been waiting expectantly for the contact ever since the adopted person reached 18 (or since 1976); on the other hand they may have based their whole life on the assumption of never being found, and may even respond in aggressive and hurtful terms through a solicitor. Most reactions will be found somewhere between these two extremes.

A frequently encountered situation is one where the birth parent is delighted that the relinquished 'child' has taken the time to search and is anxious to learn what has become of him or her in the intervening years. In such cases the parent will expect the intermediary to have many details about the adopted person and the outcome of the adoption. However, the birth parent may also be terrified of the consequences of any direct contact, especially if they have to face telling their family of a secret which has been kept, literally, for a lifetime.

The birth parent may therefore need help to decide if and when to tell the rest of their family. If the birth parent's spouse does not know of the adopted person's existence this may be a particularly difficult decision. In these cases it is best to avoid any hasty action. The birth parent should take some time to get to know the adopted person before telling anyone else. If the parent develops regular contact with their daughter or son the chances are that their spouse or children will find out by accident sooner or later if they do not tell them. The intermediary must gently point out this risk.

When the parent has a clearer idea of the type of relationship they are likely to develop with the adopted person it is easier to work out how to tell other sons and daughters. The basic information can then be supplemented with more tangible details, so that they are not just introducing the idea of an extra sibling but a real person.

No one can guarantee to any parent the reaction of their children to such a revelation. However, it may be helpful to point out that in most cases the news is welcomed rather than being the cause of distress: indeed, birth parents' children tend to feel great sympathy for the burden their parent has carried over the years. It must be appreciated however that for some people the revelation that such a major secret has been kept may cause them to doubt family openness and honesty.

The appearance of the adopted person will bring other changes too. The family pecking order will be affected: frequently the eldest child finds that they were never the eldest after all. If any one member of the birth family was especially close to the parent, they will be particularly vulnerable during any 'honeymoon' period. Disruption may also be caused if the adopted person is unused to sibling relationships and expects too much, or fails to respond appropriately to meet the norms of the new family.

The birth family will inevitably see the parent in a different light, but it will not necessarily be a less favourable one. The reactions of a previously unaware family frequently develop along similar lines to one where everything was always known so long as care is taken to ensure everyone has time to adjust to the new knowledge.

Birth parents may be afraid that the adopted person will dislike or be disappointed with them. Many birth parents are worried about their son or daugh-

ter's attitude to having been given up for adoption. They will frequently ask whether the adopted person feels rejected by them or assumes he or she was unwanted or unloved. Questions will often be asked about the outcome of the adoption, and the intermediary should ensure they have researched this with the adopted person in advance.

For some birth parents the contact may bring to the surface all the emotions they experienced when the baby had to be relinquished. The parting may well be relived and with that the anger directed at other family members who failed to provide necessary support. Similarly, if the other parent did not share responsibility, feelings of bitterness may be reawakened. If the relinquished child was conceived as a result of abuse or rape then the birth mother's distress may be much greater.

The counsellor or intermediary should ensure that all these possibilities are discussed with the adopted person so that the parent will be given sufficient time and space to resolve any problems that arise.

Handling the response

Helping the adopted person cope
As a result of the emotions experienced the birth parent may wish for immediate face-to-face contact or deny that contact can ever be made. Some will immediately appreciate the value of staged introductions and preparations, others will deny that anything can change the immediate position. This is where the intermediary will play a vital role using counselling and negotiating skills. To do this they will need to be absolutely clear about the adopted person's priorities and the type of response they will be able to handle.

Many adopted people will have insisted that they will be able to accept any response; that they only need a little information, anything else being a bonus. They will probably insist that they accept the parent's right to privacy and secrecy; that they will accept a veto on further contact; that the parent's views will be respected and they will not mind whatever the outcome. Most adopted people firmly believe this – until they have to face a rejection from their parent. Then it appears that rejection is the one thing no one is ever fully prepared to accept. At this stage the intermediary may well be accused of having 'ruined everything', with the adopted person being certain that a direct approach from them would have been completely acceptable.

Alternatively when the first approach is welcomed the adopted person may become scared and attempt to withdraw. If this happens the intermediary will need to remind them of their earlier commitment to follow through any contact. In those situations where the wishes and expectations of both parties are compatible the intermediary's task will be easier, but the bridging of the missing years should never be skipped over.

Having sent the first letter to the birth parent the intermediary may find the parent waiting on their doorstep, or besieging their switchboard first thing next morning. In other cases the wait for a response will seem interminable. Fortunately, NORCAP intermediaries have found that most relatives reply within two to three weeks. During this time the counsellor will have to support the adopted person who will probably become increasingly tense and pessimistic.

If there is no response
It will be necessary to elicit some response from the birth parent. Responsibility for parenting another person can never be entirely ended – even if that responsibility only extends to saying 'go away'. If after a month no reply has been received a further letter could be sent asking for a reply 'either way'. A reminder rarely fails – it tells the parent that this matter is not going to disappear by being ignored, and if it is unwelcome they must take action to stop it.

In the few cases where the second letter does not achieve a response, it may be necessary to resort to the telephone or a visit. At least the parent has been forewarned that someone is making enquiries and the starting point for any conversation can be an enquiry about 'the letter I sent you'. Some will immediately acknowledge an understanding of the letter whilst others will require you to spell out every detail. Whilst the intermediary's natural reaction may be to resist pressuring the parent in this way it is vital to recognise that an adopted person who has come this far is most unlikely to let the matter rest unresolved. The adopted person him or herself could exert far greater pressure on the parent.

If the enquiry is unwelcome
If a parent is unremittingly hostile to the approach the intermediary will need to try to negotiate the first priority on the adopted person's list. Some parents will agree to this in exchange for a promise 'never to contact them again', but any professional should be most cautious of giving such an undertaking. It is perhaps better to confirm that *you* accept their position and will not contact them further, but that *you* only contacted them at the request of

their son/daughter and on the basis of information supplied by that person. Therefore *you* cannot guarantee that the adopted person will not contact them again, although you will counsel him or her to accept the request the parent is making.

On the rare occasions when the parent engages a solicitor to handle their response you may also be asked for a similar undertaking. Threats of injunctions may be made but once again the counsellor can only advise and warn the adopted person. No one can actually control what another individual chooses to do.

At this point a previously reasonable adopted person who saw adoption as the parent sacrificing their feelings to ensure a happy and secure life for them may be transformed into an angry and embittered individual who sees being adopted as the first rejection and the refusal of renewed contact as the second. Although for most the initial focus of attention will be on the birth mother, attention is likely to be rapidly diverted to the birth father, siblings or other relatives if the birth mother rejects the contact. Counsellors and intermediaries should be wary: this change of direction may be an inappropriate way of handling the rejection. They should help the adopted person to work through their feelings of sorrow and bitterness before beginning another search.

If the enquiry is welcomed
Many parents will be overjoyed at the prospect of having back their baby. Whilst at an intellectual level they may appreciate that the baby is now an adult, emotionally they need the cuddly little bundle they parted with – a role the adult adopted person cannot

fulfil. The intermediary must be prepared to meet with the birth parent, and her or his family if possible, in order to work through such issues and help them come to terms with their feelings. Even if both parties are wanting direct contact and are impatient at any delay in setting up a meeting, it is well worth the intermediary risking some hostility to pace the process carefully. After all both sides have waited many years for this reunion: another few days to ensure the reunion is beneficial for everyone must be worthwhile.

Workers familiar with the placement of children may care to use their skills in life story work to good advantage prior to the reunion. Photographs and short biographies can be exchanged prior to a meeting. These help to fill in the missing years and in the birth parent's case will help them appreciate that their son or daughter is now an adult.

An exchange of letters, and possibly telephone calls, prior to a face-to-face meeting will also be useful. Indeed, some parents will only agree to limited contact such as letters, possibly via a third party. Their feelings must be respected, although it has been found that given time, and an atmosphere free from pressure, direct contact will often eventually result once confidence has grown.

Arranging a meeting
This is a very personal and private occasion. NORCAP's experience suggests that it is best if the adopted person and their birth parent can meet alone, on neutral ground, but with support available to each party both before and after the meeting (from either the counsellor or intermediary or, where appropriate, a family member or friend).

Handling the response

1. Prepare adopted person for possible responses and support them whilst awaiting reply.

2. Agree how long to wait for reply.

3. Be prepared to empathise with birth parent's position.

4. Advise on coping with feelings and reactions of other birth family members.

5. Help adopted person understand reaction of parent.

6. Follow up if no response.

7. Avoid making promises you cannot guarantee.

8. Help both parties prepare for direct contact.

9. Ensure everyone involved knows you are available to help further.

The actual meeting should be in a setting where neither emotional nor cool behaviour will appear unusual. A railway station or airport provides an ideal location – people continually coming and going, individuals waiting and watching expectantly. This leaves them free to rush towards one another and embrace or to approach coolly and shake hands. In such locations a cafe and toilets are available which may be necessary if nervous people are waiting around.

Ideally a park or gallery would be available nearby where they can wander, chatting or not as they feel inclined. Having something other than each other to focus on will help avoid embarrassing silences.

If at all possible the first meeting should be arranged so that neither party has to travel a considerable distance whilst the other has the advantage of being on home ground. An office location is rarely appropriate (although it may be in some circumstances: Family Care in Scotland, as the 'bridge' which brought the two sides together, is often used by birth parents and adopted people as a 'safe' meeting place). Neither party's home should be used unless the parent is so elderly and infirm that a meeting cannot be achieved any other way.

Much will already have been done to help the participants prepare for the event, but both parties need to be aware that they are likely to experience considerable reaction to this meeting. Among those reported are feelings akin to post-natal depression. The comparison can clearly be seen: preparation over a period of several months culminating in a key event (the first meeting) which results in all those pent-up emotions being dissipated; followed by concern over how to handle the ongoing relationship and fears about the ability to meet the demands that may be made of them. Another possibility is a 'honeymoon' phase when other relationships will be temporarily excluded and at risk.

Both parties should be offered the opportunity to discuss their reactions to the meeting. It is likely that the adopted person will want to recount every detail of the meeting to the counsellor, and anyone else prepared to listen! However, if things have not gone according to plan, the counsellor will need to offer a sympathetic ear and, where necessary, advice and help to solve any problems.

Once the new relationship is established most parties will take great care to maintain it, everyone being careful not to cause offence or to annoy or distress any other party. This does not reflect normal family relationships and eventually there will be a disagreement or quarrel. Everyone may then be afraid that the relationship is ended, so the counsellor and/or intermediary should ensure that all are aware that the test of the reunion is not how long they can avoid disagreement but how well they can handle the difficulty and resolve any conflict. Only then can anyone claim the relationship is moving towards normality.

The counsellor may not be involved beyond this stage, but before withdrawing he or she should ensure everyone is aware that further help can be given if ever needed.

Finally, the one person who the counsellor is unlikely to have thought too much about throughout the entire birth records counselling process is her or himself. But such work is often demanding and emotionally draining, and counsellors should not be afraid to arrange an opportunity for themselves to share their own responses and feelings with another worker.

✓ CHECKLIST 10

Arranging a meeting

1. Arrange and confirm venue and time.

2. Identify potential for other activity at meeting place.

3. Prepare both parties for the meeting by discussing possible reactions.

4. Check both parties will have support available.

5. Arrange meetings/telephone calls to discuss reactions.

6. Be prepared for problem-solving and crisis intervention.

7. Remind both parties of the availability of post-reunion support.

8. Arrange support and opportunity to unload for self.

Appendices

Useful organisations and addresses

Adoption Counselling Centre (Family Care)
21 Castle Street
Edinburgh EH2 3DN
Telephone: 031-225 3666
Offers advice, counselling and group work to adopted people, adoptive parents and birth parents, advice and counselling to siblings, and training and consultancy to workers. Undertakes searches on behalf of adopted people and offers an intermediary service. Holds Scottish Adoption Registry (list of adoptions in Scotland) and runs Birth Link Register.

British Agencies for Adoption & Fostering
(Head Office)
11 Southwark Street
London SE1 1RQ
Telephone: 071-407 8800
BAAF has consultants at head office and at each of its regional centres. BAAF's Black Issues Project consultants can be contacted at head office.

General Register Office (England and Wales)
Address for postal applications for birth records information and for Adoption Contact Register:
General Register Office (Adoptions Section)
Smedley Hydro
Trafalgar Road
Southport
Merseyside PR8 2HH
Telephone: 0704-69824
Address for indexes of all births and marriages in England and Wales:
General Register Office
St Catherine's House
10 Kingsway
London WC2 6JP
Telephone: 071-242 0262

General Register Office (Northern Ireland)
Oxford House
49-55 Chichester Street
Belfast BT1 4HL
Telephone: 0232-235211

General Register Office (Republic of Ireland)
8-11 Lombard Street East
Dublin 2

General Register Office (Scotland)
New Register House
Princes Street
Edinburgh EH1 3YT
Telephone: 031-334 0380
Holds adoption, birth, death and marriage certificate records.

National Organisation for the Counselling of Adoptees & Parents (NORCAP)
3 New High Street
Headington
Oxford OX3 7AJ
Telephone: 0865-750554

Offers searching advice, counselling, and intermediary service, plus the opportunity to join local groups throughout England and Wales. Provides network of local volunteer helpers known as Contact Leaders who are available to members. Also arranges supported 'search days' at the General Register Office. Publishes quarterly newsletter which includes members' personal stories and news items. Maintains its own adoption contact register.

Natural Parents' Support Group
Queries from workers and counsellors to:
Doreen Ward
10 Alandale Crescent
Garforth
Leeds LS25 1DH
Natural parents should write to:
Jan Hanmer
3 Alder Grove
Normanton
West Yorkshire WF6 1LF
Support group run by and for people who parted with a child for adoption.

Parent to Parent Information on Adoption Services (PPIAS)
Lower Boddington
Daventry
Northamptonshire NN11 6YB
Telephone: 0327-60295
Self-help group offering support, advice and encouragement for prospective and existing adopters and permanent substitute families. Has 130 local co-ordinators who give support and advice to prospective and existing adopters. Produces quarterly newsletter.

Post-Adoption Centre
8 Torriano Mews
Torriano Avenue
London NW5 2RZ
Telephone: 071-284 0555

Provides advice, counselling and group activities for all individuals involved in adoption – adopted people, adoptive parents and birth families (fees for extended work charged on sliding scale according to income). Workshops held for groups of individuals and professionals on wide range of issues (apply to Centre for forthcoming programme). Also offers specialist consultancy service for professionals and publishes research documents and discussion papers. Their professional team includes black workers and is widely experienced in all aspects of adoption.

Post Adoption Services
2nd Floor
Lloyds House
22 Lloyd Street
Manchester M2 5WA
Telephone: 061-839 4930
Offers information, advice, counselling and support to anyone who has been touched by adoption.

ROOTS
contact: Olga and Lloyd Rains
Box 94
Hyde Park
Ontario
Canada NOM 120
Agency specialising in tracing Canadian servicemen.

Scottish Adoption Advice Service
16 Sandyford Place
Glasgow G3 7NB
Telephone: 041-339 0772
Agency offering counselling, advice and support. Telephone advice service between 2.00pm and 7.00pm on Wednesdays.

Scottish Record Office
General Register House
2 Princes Street
Edinburgh EH1 3YY

Telephone: 031-556 6585
Holds court records, including adoption processes (papers held by the court in connection with an adoption).

Somerset House
The Strand
London WC2
Holds microfilmed records of divorces and the Probate Register for England and Wales.

Trans-Atlantic Children's Enterprise (TRACE)
contact: Sophia Byrne
11 St Tewdrick's Place
Methern
Nr Chepstow
Gwent NP6 6JW
Self-help group which gives advice on finding the fathers of children born as a result of liaisons between American GIs and British women.

Triangle
8 Kingston Road
West Bridgeford
Nottingham
Organisation run by experienced adoption worker providing service for people involved in adoption able to attend group and individual sessions in Nottingham. Close links with The Child Migrant Trust, a charity offering assistance to individuals involved in the child migration schemes which operated until the 1960s. Triangle would be able to give expert advice to any adopted person who found links to family overseas.

Appendix 2
**Suggested further reading on adoption
and searching**

Austin J (ed) *Adoption: the inside story*
Barn Owl Books, 1987
A collection of articles from early
PPIAS (Parent to Parent Information on
Adoption Services) newsletters giving a
comprehensive view of adoption from
the point of view of all the participants
– adopters, adopted people and birth
relatives.

Krementz J *How it feels to be adopted*
New York: Knopf, 1988
Written following conversations between the author and a variety of
young Americans who had been adopted, this book gives personal insights
into the experiences and responses to
their adoption of young adopted people.

Lifton B J *Lost and found* New York:
Harper & Row, 1988
An in-depth study of the psychological
issues faced by adopted people and
others separated from a parent and
denied knowledge of their origins.

Searching for family connections NOR-
CAP, 1984 (revised 1988)
A detailed, step-by-step guide to the
birth records search, based on the experience of those who have been through
it themselves.

*Shared experience: collected stories
from 'NORCAP News' 1-12* NORCAP,
1986
A collection of articles from early NOR-
CAP newsletters which relay personal
experiences of searching, contacting
and meeting with birth relatives.

Appendix 3
Bibliography and suggested further reading for counsellors

Bean P (ed) *Adoption: essays in social policy, law and sociology* Tavistock Publications, 1984
Includes a chapter on obtaining birth certificates by John Triseliotis and another on growing up adopted by Martin Shaw. Concise and invaluable research-based information for counsellors.

Burnell A and Fitsell A *Feeding the hungry ghost* Post-Adoption Centre, 1990
A brief paper written by counsellors at the Post-Adoption Centre, based on their work with adopted people seeking information about their families of origin.

Day C and Leeding A *Access to birth records* ABAFA, 1980
Reports on a research study of the first applicants for birth records counselling in England and Wales in the late 1970s.

Haimes E and Timms N *Adoption, identity and social policy* Gower, 1985
Based on research conducted for the Department of Health in the mid-1980s into birth records counselling as seen by counsellors and adopted people. The underlying link with self-identity is explored in depth.

Hodgkins P *Adopted adults: their relationship with their birth and adoptive family* NORCAP, 1987
Research report into the reunions of 180 adopted adults with birth relatives. Also examines the relationship with adoptive families and explores links between satisfaction with the adopted family and the wish to contact birth relatives.

Rayner L *The adopted child comes of age* George Allen & Unwin, 1980
A retrospective study of adoptive families and the development and adjustment of adopted people.

Shekleton J *A glimpse through the looking glass* Post-Adoption Centre, 1990
Discussion paper offering poignant insights into the personal experiences of transracially adopted adults, and highlighting their intense need to define 'self'.

Stafford G *Where to find adoption records: a guide for counsellors* BAAF, 1985
An essential reference book for all birth records counsellors, providing details of the availability of adoption records and comprehensive details of adoption agencies and maternity, mother-and-baby and shelter homes both past and present.

Triseliotis J *In search of origins* Routledge & Kegan Paul, 1973
Early research into the tracing of birth relatives by adopted people in Scotland which was influential in the debate concerning the granting of access to birth records in England and Wales.

Walby C and Symons B *Who am I? - identity, adoption and human fertilisation* BAAF, 1990
Draws parallels between the experiences of adopted people and the needs of people born as a result of human fertilisation techniques. Explores the history and development of adoption, with particular reference to research around issues of identity and origins, and emphasises the reasons behind the search among adopted people and others not brought up by their genetic parents for a sense of identity.

Checklist for birth records counsellors

The checklists in this appendix may be photocopied by individuals for personal use. Unauthorised reproduction of these exercises by any other means, or in any other form, is illegal.

✓ CHECKLIST 1

Arranging the first interview (England, Wales and Northern Ireland)

1. Receive request for counselling from Registrar General and appoint appropriate counsellor.

2. Send acknowledgement to applicant.

3. Offer appointment. Indicate that:
   • the interview is not a testing situation
   • the applicant will be given their birth name and location
   • they are welcome to bring a 'supporter'
   • they may bring any information they already hold.

4. Note appointment in diary.

5. Ensure an interview room is available.

✓ CHECKLIST 2

Preparing for the first interview (England, Wales and Northern Ireland)

1. Read carefully the information received from the Registrar General.

2. Are placement records to hand?

   No – go to 3

   Yes – go to 5

3. Try to identify placement agency.

4. Establish availability of any addresses.

5. Check addresses with current register of electors.

6. Prepare summary of information.

7. If agency file already supplied, photocopy documents to give to the adopted person at the interview.

✓ CHECKLIST 1

Arranging the first interview (Scotland)

1. Receive request for counselling which the adopted person may make by letter, on the telephone or in person.

2. Appoint an appropriate counsellor.

3. Arrange interview. Indicate that the adopted person may bring a supporter and should bring any information they already hold.

4. Note appointment in diary.

5. Ensure an interview room is available.

✓ CHECKLIST 2

Preparing for the first interview (Scotland)

1. Read or consider carefully any information supplied by the adopted person and any indication of the reasons they are seeking counselling.

2. Check whether any information or records are immediately available.

   If so:

3. Prepare summary of information.

4. Photocopy documents to give to the adopted person at the interview.

☑ CHECKLIST 3

The statutory interview (England, Wales and Northern Ireland)

1. Check identification of applicant.

2. Give applicant form containing their birth records information.

3. Identify agency involved AND/OR offer applicant form to apply to court for this information.

4. Advise applicant you have shared all information available to you OR explain you have further information to hand which you will share after further counselling.

5. Give applicant opportunity to discuss matters relating to his or her adoption, including aims and expectations for moving the enquiry forward.

6. Advise applicant about adoption contact registers.

7. Offer to arrange an intermediary.

8. Invite applicant to further interview.

9. Agree with applicant how/when next session will be arranged.

10. Identify tasks for completion prior to next session.
   Applicant:
   • Apply for original birth certificate.
   • Apply for information from court.
   • Advise counsellor when details available.
   • List everything ever told/heard about birth family.
   Counsellor:
   • Identify current location of records.
   • Request loan of file.
   • Make time and venue available for second session.

11. Return to Registrar General the form showing interview has taken place.

☑ CHECKLIST 3

The first interview (Scotland)

1. Check identification of applicant.

2. Identify agency involved and/or court which made the adoption order. Ensure applicant is aware they are entitled to see the court process.

3. Share any information available to you or explain you have further information to hand which you will share after further counselling.

4. Give applicant opportunity to discuss any matters relating to his or her adoption, including aims and expectations for moving the enquiry forward.

5. Offer to arrange an intermediary.

6. Invite applicant to further interview.

7. Agree with applicant how/when next session will be arranged.

8. Identify tasks for completion prior to next session.
   Applicant:
   • Arrange to read court process and note details.
   • Advise counsellor of relevant details.
   • List everything ever told/heard about birth family.
   Counsellor:
   • Identify current location of agency records.
   • Request loan of file.
   • Make time and venue available for second session.

✓ CHECKLIST 4

What the counsellor can do

1. Obtain adoption file and any extra papers from:
   - placement agency
   - supervising authority
   - organisation that assisted birth mother
   - any other identified source.

2. Prepare summary for adopted person.

3. Negotiate and agree release of original letters and photographs to adopted person and replace in file with good photocopies.

✓ CHECKLIST 5

The second interview

1. Has enough time been given to talking things through?

2. Discuss acceptable/risky methods of searching.

3. Provide advice/guidelines on searching; suggest purchase of *Searching for family connections.*

4. Recommend that adopted person works quite slowly so as to have time to absorb and think over each discovery made.

5. Discuss the possibility that the birth parent may have died.

6. Stress that you are available for advice/further meetings as the search progresses.

7. Give further reminder of the need for an intermediary.

✓ CHECKLIST 6

What to do when the search is successful

1. Talk through searching methods and results.

2. Acknowledge impact of information gained.

3. Carefully check research. Has correct person been found?

4. What assumptions are being made about the circumstances of the adoption, the birth mother, etc?

5. Identify adopted person's current aims and objectives.

✓ CHECKLIST 7

Areas to be explored prior to initiating contact

1. Adopted person's responsibilities as a result of initiating contact.

2. Identifying who will know about the adoption.

3. Comparison of adopted person's and birth family's lifestyles.

4. Discussion of racial and cultural issues in transracial adoptions.

5. Coping with likely impact on the birth family.

6. Risks of relationship developing sexually.

7. Meeting with adopted person's own family.

8. Position with regard to adoptive parents.

] CHECKLIST 8

How to make contact

] Decide method in light of circumstances.

] Keep letter simple; don't inadvertently give away the letter's purpose in the designation or letterhead.

] Ensure that other commitments will not unduly delay dealing with any response.

] CHECKLIST 9

Handling the response

] Prepare adopted person for possible responses and support them whilst awaiting reply.

] Agree how long to wait for reply.

] Be prepared to empathise with birth parent's position.

] Advise on coping with feelings and reactions of other birth family members.

] Help adopted person understand reaction of parent.

] Follow up if no response.

] Avoid making promises you cannot guarantee.

] Help both parties prepare for direct contact.

] Ensure everyone involved knows you are available to help further.

✓ CHECKLIST 10

Arranging a meeting

1 Arrange and confirm venue and time.

2 Identify potential for other activity at meeting place.

3 Prepare both parties for the meeting by discussing possible reactions.

4 Check both parties will have support available.

5 Arrange meetings/telephone calls to discuss reactions.

6 Be prepared for problem-solving and crisis intervention.

7 Remind both parties of the availability of post-reunion support.

8 Arrange support and opportunity to unload for self.
